PENGUIN

THE MIRROR OF

DICK DAVIS is the foremost English-speaking scholar of medieval Persian poetry in the West and "our finest translator of Persian poetry" (*The Times Literary Supplement*). A fellow of the Royal Society of Literature and an emeritus professor of Persian at Ohio State University, he has published more than twenty books, including *Love in Another Language: Collected Poems and Selected Translations.* His other translations from Persian include *The Conference of the Birds*; *Vis and Ramin*; *Layli and Majnun*; *Faces of Love: Hafez and the Poets of Shiraz*; and *Shahnameh: The Persian Book of Kings*, one of *The Washington Post*'s ten best books of 2006. Davis lives in Columbus, Ohio.

The Mirror of My Heart

A THOUSAND YEARS OF
PERSIAN POETRY BY WOMEN

Translated with an Introduction and Notes by
DICK DAVIS

PENGUIN BOOKS

PENGUIN BOOKS
An imprint of Penguin Random House LLC
penguinrandomhouse.com

First published in the United States of America by Mage Publishers 2019
Published in Penguin Books 2021

LIBRARY OF CONGRESS CATALOGING-IN-PUBLICATION DATA
Names: Davis, Dick, 1945– translator.
Title: The mirror of my heart : a thousand years of Persian poetry by
women / translated with an introduction and notes by Dick Davis.
Description: New York : Penguin Books, 2021. |
Includes bibliographical references.
Identifiers: LCCN 2020046588 (print) | LCCN 2020046589 (ebook) |
ISBN 9780143135616 (paperback) | ISBN 9780525507260 (ebook)
Subjects: LCSH: Persian poetry—Women authors.
Classification: LCC PK6434.5.W64 M57 2021 (print) |
LCC PK6434.5.W64 (ebook) | DDC 891/.55100899287—dc23
LC record available at https://lccn.loc.gov/2020046588
LC ebook record available at https://lccn.loc.gov/2020046589

Printed in the United States of America

Set in Bembo Std

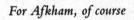

For Afkham, of course

The liberating space that was Persian poetry . . . allowed subversive—indeed, heretical—expressions forbidden in any other media. Skepticism, even about the most sacred beliefs and duties, and sneering at the authorities, religious and political, was tolerated as the fruit of poetic imagination.

—Abbas Amanat[1]

Woman's crime in our country is to be a woman.

—Alam Taj (Zhaleh), Iranian poet (1883–1947)[2]

Contents

THE MIRROR OF MY HEART

The Poets

FROM THE 1800s TO THE PRESENT

Introduction

A significant feature of Persian poetry that distinguishes it from most verse written in a European language is that almost all of it—from the earliest poems, written over a thousand years ago, to the present day—remains relatively accessible to a contemporary speaker of the language. The seventeenth-century English poet Edmund Waller bemoaned the fact that, already, his contemporaries could no longer easily read the works of the fourteenth-century poet Chaucer:

> But who can hope his lines should long
> Last in a daily changing tongue . . .
> We write in sand, our language grows,
> And like the tide our work o'erflows.
>
> Chaucer his sense can only boast,
> The glory of his numbers lost!*

And as if to confirm Waller's complaint, it was in Waller's lifetime that passages from Chaucer were first "translated" into contemporary English, by Dryden. The Persian language, especially its literary form, has remained far more stable over

---

*Edmund Waller, *Seventeenth Century English Minor Poets*, ed. Anne Ferry (New York: 1964), p. 143.

the past millennium than is true of most European languages. There have been some changes of vocabulary and grammar, but by Western standards they are minor: a modern-day Iranian can read the works of the tenth-century poet Ferdowsi with about the same ease as a modern-day English speaker can read those of seventeenth-century authors such as Waller and Dryden; there are some difficulties for a non-specialist in the period, but they do not obscure what is usually the obvious sense and rhetorical force of any given passage. A side-effect of the fact that poems from centuries ago can seem and sound relatively "contemporary" to the Persian reader is that such poems could be—and were—taken as models by poets from a much later date, and this in turn has led to a quite extraordinary continuity of poetic rhetoric from the earliest poems until at least the mid nineteenth century, and even beyond that period.

There is perhaps something else at work in this rhetorical continuity: all poetry is artificial in its language, but poetry in English has frequently tended to aim at "language really used by men," as Wordsworth put it,* and when this is the case it tries, as far as possible, to disguise its artifice; by contrast pre-modern† Persian poetry tends to display, and delight in, its artifice. To say a poem in English sounds "artificial" is to condemn it; the same remark about a pre-modern Persian poem could well elicit the

---

* Wordsworth, "Preface to *Lyrical Ballads*," in *Poets on Poetry*, ed. Charles Norman (New York: 1962), p. 138.

† "Pre-modern" is here used to refer to Persian poetry written in the "classical" metrical system (*aruz*) in which virtually all Persian poetry was written before the mid-twentieth century. Though a number of poets still use this system, sometimes in a modified form, the last major woman poet to have used it exclusively was Parvin Etesami (1907–1941).

response "Of course it does; it's a poem, isn't it?" And so the fact that a particular metaphor or rhetorical trope has been used by many other poets, and is thought of as intrinsically "poetic" rather than as colloquial, is not so much a barrier to its continued use as a validation of it. The poets Ayyuqi (tenth–eleventh centuries) and Nezami (twelfth century) both say that the poet is like the woman who tends to a bride's physical appearance before her wedding; that is, the poet uses his or her skill and artifice to make the subject as dazzlingly beautiful as possible. Other common metaphors used by poets themselves to describe poetry are that it is something woven, such as brocade, or a piece of jewelry, such as a pearl necklace. All three of these metaphors emphasize the aesthetic, artificial, fabricated, and artisanal nature of the craft, rather than, say, its sincerity or its truth-telling qualities as they are foregrounded in much Western poetry ("to hold . . . the mirror up to nature," as Shakespeare's Hamlet says).

To indicate something of the density and complexity of this artifice in pre-modern Persian poetry, here is a translation of a very early poem that is made up almost entirely of motifs that belonged to a common stock widely utilized by other poets for centuries to come. The poem is by the tenth-century poet Rabe'eh, who, as is appropriate for this volume, is the earliest-known woman poet to write in Persian:

> The garden shows so many flowers, as though
> Mani had painted their resplendent glow
>
> Dawn's breezes never bore Tibetan musk,
> How is the world so musky when they blow?

Are Majnun's eyes within the clouds, that they
Shed Layli's cheeks' hue on each rose below?

Like wine within an agate glass, his tears
Have filled each tulip with their crimson glow

Raise up the wine bowl, raise it generously
Since bad luck dogs deniers who say "No"

Narcissi glow with silver and with gold
It's Kasra's crown their shining petals show

Like nuns in purple cowls the violets bloom
Do they turn into Christians as they grow? (pp. 3–4)

The poem is a *baharieh*—that is, a poem welcoming the spring, a form that is still, a thousand years later, a recognized category of Persian poetry—and it is set in the archetypal beautiful place for Persian culture, the *locus amoenus* to end them all, a garden. But what is "Mani," the third-century founder of the religion of Manicheism, doing in the poem? In Persian lore he was also a painter whose beautiful paintings looked so true to life that they deceived both people and animals, and this accounts for "painted" in the second line. Because the flowers are compared to Mani's paintings, this means they must be very beautiful, and Persian poetry takes it for granted that beauty is a major concern of every civilized person. And something else is also going on here: Mani was the founder of a pre-Islamic religion seen as a heresy by Moslems, and yet he is mentioned, apparently favorably, in a poem written by someone we presume to be a Moslem. Persian poetry often mentions religions other than Islam, and in short lyric poems, like this one, the reference is almost always either favorable or neutral; it virtually never implies condemnation (this is less true of long didactic poems, in which religions other than Islam are sometimes implicitly or explicitly condemned). This suggests that Persian lyric poetry perhaps sees itself as somewhat at odds with an exclusively Islamic world-view, or at least as not prepared to denigrate other religions in its favor, and this is indeed the case. Persian lyric poetry is in general welcomingly receptive to both the pre-Islamic past and non-Islamic faiths. The implication is that there is not one sole Truth applicable at all times to all people; that other ways of being, from the past or as an adherent of another faith, can be considered to be equally valid. Later on, such references were read as allegorical (the mention of a figure from another religion, for example, was seen as a metaphor for one who transmits mystical knowledge—that is, a knowledge outside of the mainstream of "orthodox" Islam), and in later poems they often *are* allegorical, but they were meant quite literally, for themselves, in Rabe'eh's poems, as they were in the poems of her contemporaries and of many subsequent poets.

Regarded as particularly refreshing and pleasant, the cool breeze of dawn, referred to in the second stanza of the poem, is a constituent of the idealized landscapes of much Persian poetry. This breeze apparently brings the scent of musk, the most valued and expensive of medieval perfumes, and again we see that we are being presented with an idealized situation in which everything, including the scented air, is as beguilingly charming and special as possible. The musk comes from Tibet, a remote and exotic place for the speaker, and the poem momentarily opens on a distant, almost fabulous, reality, as with the mention of Mani. Here the musk is a metaphor for the scent of the garden's flowers as it is diffused by the breeze, the logic being that musk is the most precious perfume, so the flowers in this idealized garden share its scent, and this rare, idealized loveliness provokes wonder in the speaker. Wonder at what seems perfect (a garden, a person, a state of mind—usually love or grief), or extreme to the point of unreality, is a very commonly evoked effect in Persian poetry.

Next we come to Layli and Majnun, star-crossed lovers from an originally seventh-century Arabic tale that quickly spread all over the Islamic world. Since he is a tragic figure, unable to be united with his beloved, Majnun is often represented as weeping and this is why he is mentioned in the third stanza of the poem as being "within the clouds"—he is weeping the dew onto the flowers below him (dew continues the implication that the poem is describing a scene in the early morning, which is considered to be the loveliest and most refreshing time of day). Layli's cheeks are imagined as red, either as an indication of her beauty or of her flushed, bewildered distress, or both, so Majnun's tears, which are the same color as her cheeks, are red. The conceit is that the tears are bloody, indicating that Majnun has wept so long and so hard that his eyes are injured and he weeps blood; with the same implication of relentless injurious weeping, tears are almost always referred to as red in pre-modern Persian verse (an exception is when they are compared to pearls). So the roses are red because Majnun has wept his red tears onto them. The metaphor is continued in the next stanza, in which tulips are compared to wine glasses (short wild tulips, whose shape is easy to imagine as like that of a wine glass, are meant), and in which the dew/bloody tears present in these wine glasses is implicitly being compared to red wine. The association of red flowers (almost always roses or tulips), bloody tears, and wine is common in Persian verse, with any one of the three being able to stand in metaphorically for either of the other two.

Having implied the presence of wine, Rabe'eh now runs with the idea and brings literal wine into the poem, admonishing the reader (in Rabe'eh's time more likely a listener, as lyric poetry was meant to be performed rather than silently read) to drink deeply, and to ignore those who would censor such behavior. The obvious candidates for people who would find fault in this way are strictly orthodox Moslems, as the drinking of wine is forbidden by Islam. This trope, of the wine drinker criticized by the strictly orthodox (often characterized as being hypocrites), with the poet explicitly siding with the drinker against the orthodox, became extremely common in Persian lyric verse. Again we see behavior that is at odds with strict Islamic norms being celebrated, and again we find later generations taking the trope as an elaborate metaphor for Sufi (mystical) experience (wine is the mystical knowledge or practice which brings about the "drunkenness" of mystical experience). This is true of later Persian poetry, and from the late fifteenth century onward, mention of wine in a poem *is*, as often as not, allegorical. However, this "Sufification" of the vocabulary of secular Persian poetry had not even begun in Rabe'eh's time, and there can be no doubt that she is talking about literal wine here.

As the poem is written to welcome the coming of spring, it would be associated in the minds of its first readers/auditors with Nowruz, the pre-Islamic festival held at the spring equinox, which heralds the Persian New Year. This festival is still celebrated in Iran and is perhaps the only festival in which all Iranians, whatever faith they profess, participate. Wine was drunk in the pre-Islamic celebrations of Nowruz, and because of this and similar ceremonies, wine retained its association with pre-Islamic Iran, and the pre-Islamic religion of Iran, Zoroastrianism. The mention of wine drunk in spring therefore introduces another non-Islamic religion into the poem, not explicitly but by an implication any educated Iranian reader would recognize. Also, by implication, the line that dismisses those who criticize the drinking of wine, who are most likely to be orthodox Moslems, suggests a tension between the religion that condemns wine (Islam) and the religion that celebrates it (Zoroastrianism). The opposition does not merely consist of refraining from wine or drinking it, but by extension of celebrating worldly pleasures or of condemning them; many Persian poems implicitly associate worldly pleasures such as wine drinking with Zoroastrianism and pre-Islamic Iran, and the conjunction of the two is contrasted with Islam, which is often characterized, in poetry at least, as condemning such pleasures. This tacit association of pre-Islamic Iran with Zoroastrianism and pleasurable celebration leads us to the poem's next lines, which include a mention of "Kasra."

Kasra is a corruption of "Khosrow" and refers to the pre-Islamic king Khosrow I, also known as Anushirvan ("Of Immortal Soul"), who ruled Iran from 531 to 579 CE, and was one of the most successful of the pre-Islamic kings, to the extent that his reign was remembered as a golden age of justice and prosperity. Rabe'eh has made specific the suggestion of pre-Islamic Iran, implied by the lines on wine, by alluding to what was in folk memory the country's most splendid imperial moment. That it is the imperial aspect of his reign that is emphasized is indicated by the reference to the gold and silver of his crown, to which the color of the garden's narcissi is compared. Two related tropes common to Persian verse are present here: one is the lost glory of Iran's imperial past; and the other is that all glory is fleeting, that dynasties die and the sites of their splendor return to nature.

The last two lines bring the poem back to the present, but not to the immediate circumstances of Rabe'eh's daily life, which will of course have been Moslem; by referring to Christian nuns, the poem ends by evoking another non-Islamic religion. She is referring to something that is known to her but absent from her own life's immediate Moslem circumstances, something which she would not have experienced directly, just as she would not have known the Zoroastrian glories of Kasra's reign; the poem ends by reaching out to two "exotic" realities, one from the past and one from another religious community, that are nevertheless imaginatively present for the poet. And we can say that, if the poem is by Rabe'eh, it also ends with what looks like an approving, or at least certainly not disapproving and perhaps affectionate, smile for her non-Moslem sisters. If the poem is by Rabe'eh, that is, because the last thing it shares with many other short Persian poems is that it has been mistakenly attributed to at least two other poets of the early medieval period, Rudaki and Suzani-ye Samarqandi. Different manuscripts attribute a large number of short Persian poems to different authors and the authorship of many poems, particularly from the earliest periods, remains doubtful; in this case, though, the scholarly consensus is that the poem is by Rabe'eh.

And so, packed into one short poem, we have: spring, a garden, the breeze at dawn, the most valued medieval perfume (musk), an evocation of a distant land (Tibet), wonder at an ideally beautiful situation, a reference to a tragic Arab love story, blood-red tears, non-judgmental references to two non-Islamic faiths (Manicheism and Christianity) and the evocation of a third (Zoroastrianism), a reference to a glorious pre-Islamic Persian king, the admonition to drink wine, and a kind of flippant contempt for those who would frown on this. The poem is superficially a simple celebration of the coming of spring, and this is a perfectly legitimate way to read it, but it is implicitly and deliberately entangled in a complicated mesh of cultural references that would be obvious to its original audience and to later readers from the same culture but which can be elusive for a reader from another cultural tradition. All of these poetic strategies, tropes, and metaphors constantly recur in Persian poetry as it was written for a thousand years subsequent to Rabe'eh's poem.

The Medieval Period

Persian poetry begins in the tenth century and, as we have seen, Rabe'eh was one of its earliest practitioners. Iran had been conquered by an Arab invasion that brought the then new religion of Islam to the country in the seventh century, and the culture of Iran, including its language, was radically transformed by this conquest. Here an analogy with a somewhat similar Western cultural transformation may perhaps be useful. England was conquered in the eleventh century by the Norman French, and French culture, and the French language, dominated the court and virtually every level of society above the peasantry for the next three centuries. In the fourteenth century, Chaucer is one of the first, and certainly the greatest among his contemporaries, of the poets to write in the new form of English, which was an amalgam of Anglo-Saxon and French. Like Rabe'eh's verse, his too seems to us simple and direct, and in the nineteenth century Chaucer's verse was sometimes referred to as being written in the "springtime" of British poetry, with all the connotations of newness, freshness, and innocence the word implies. But Chaucer's verse, like Rabe'eh's, is immensely sophisticated beneath its beguilingly charming surface, and it is written very consciously in the shadow of the French culture and language, which had been brought by Britain's conquerors three centuries before; indeed, Chaucer began his career as a poet with a partial translation of the most popular French long poem of the age, *Le Roman de la Rose*. Both Chaucer and Rabe'eh wrote at a time when a new indigenous literary culture was emerging from the shadow of a linguistic and cultural conquest that had occurred three centuries before their own time. Both are learned poets who paradoxically seem in many ways much more innocent and untutored than their successors, but this "innocence" is built on an urbane awareness of a complex literary culture to which their own poetry is consciously indebted but from which it is providing as it were a literary way out, with the founding of a new indigenous poetry.

Like Chaucer's, Rabe'eh's is a simplicity that hides a great deal of learning and sophistication. For example, she is, as far as we know, the first Persian poet to write macaronic verse—that is, verse that is written in two languages, usually in alternating lines; in Rabe'eh's case the alternating lines are in Arabic and Persian. This implies fluency in Arabic, and what we know of her biography seems relevant here. Her family name indicates an Arab origin at a time when the court language of most Persian princedoms (her father was just such a local prince, in Balkh) was in the process of changing from Arabic to Persian, which means that she was almost certainly bilingual. Her father's name was K'ab and her own name as it appears in early sources is Rabe'eh bint K'ab; her brother's name was Hareth. All three names are Arabic, and indeed the family claimed descent from Arab immigrants who had established a petty kingdom centered on Balkh in what is now northern Afghanistan.

Rabe'eh appears at the beginning of the revival of Persian poetry after the "two centuries of silence" (the phrase was coined by the twentieth-century Iranian scholar Abdolhossein Zarrinkub) that ensued after the Arab/Islamic conquest of the seventh century. Referring to English literature in particular but implying literature in general, the eighteenth-century literary historian Thomas Warton pointed out that after a "dark ages" in which learning and literacy are largely lost, at least in their native linguistic form, "writers are chiefly employed in imparting the ideas of other languages into their own."* In the case of Rabe'eh's generation, the "other language" in question was obviously Arabic; the great Italian Persianist Alessandro Bausani wrote of this earliest period in the revival of Persian poetry, "We are in the presence of . . . a linguistic Iranization of Arabic conceptual traditions and lyric conventions."† The language still used to describe Persian poetry confirms its early debt to Arabic: virtually every word descriptive of poetic rhetoric in Persian (meter, rhyme, metaphor, pun, etc.) is Arabic.

Let us consider Rabe'eh's position: she grows up at a provincial court where we can presume she had access to whatever literary learning was available in her time and place, as is attested by her surviving poems; she is bilingual in Arabic and Persian as her macaronic poems indicate; she lives at a moment when Persian poetry is effecting a rebirth by, as Bausani says, "a linguistic Iranization of Arabic conceptual traditions and lyric conventions"; and given the fact that she uses them, her familiarity with the rules and tropes of Arabic versification can be taken for granted. These circumstances render her almost uniquely able to effect the transfer of Arabic poetic conventions to Persian verse. This suggests that Rabe'eh was not merely a woman who happened to write verse at the moment when Persian poetry was being reborn, but that her role in this revival was crucial and perhaps decisive. Her circumstances and achievement indicate that she was someone whose example made possible the revival of Persian poetry, at least in terms of its major non-Persian model. This is not at all to imply that she was the only person who did

_____

* Thomas Warton, *The History of English Poetry, from the Close of the Eleventh to the Commencement of the Eighteenth Century* (London: 1781), p. 226.

† A. Bausani, *Storia della letteratura persiana* (Milan: 1960), p. 310.

this, but she was certainly in a privileged, influential position and well qualified to contribute to this process. We can see her as an instigator, someone who pointed the way in which Persian verse was to develop, rather than as just one of the small number of Persian poets who happened to be writing at this time, and one who happened to be a woman.

Rabe'eh was a court poet, as were virtually all medieval Persian poets (the exceptions were poets whose main subject was Sufism, although Sufis were sometimes court poets too). But there is a crucial difference between her and almost all of her male counterparts. The men were professional poets, dependent on the largesse of the prince or of the courtiers at the court at which they worked. Rabe'eh was a princess, not a court employee, and as such it's unlikely that she was paid for her poetry, or if she did receive some kind of emolument or reward for her poems, this wasn't something she depended on for her livelihood. So she was, in the literal sense, an amateur poet—that is, someone who wrote poetry because she wished to do so, not as a paid profession. Many of the women poets who followed in Rabe'eh's footsteps, princesses or aristocrats like her, were also "amateur" poets in this sense, members rather than employees of a ruling family. When we do find women poets later on who were employed by noble families, they were virtually never employed as poets; they were usually entertainers of some kind, sometimes courtesans, employed not for their poetry but for other skills and for their personal charms.

Yet it has to be said that although we find women poets writing in Persian in almost every generation from Rabe'eh on, their number is comparatively small when compared with that of their male contemporaries. It is, however, on a par with the relatively small number of women poets to be found in most cultures during the pre-modern period (perhaps the major exceptions are the cultures of medieval China and Japan, both of which produced a goodly number of women poets), and at certain times for particular cultures—such as English literary culture during the Middle Ages—it considerably exceeds that number.

Pre-modern Persian poetry can be broadly divided into three different kinds: long narrative poems, short lyric poems, and epigrams. There are no surviving long narrative poems by women from the pre-modern period; so far as women poets are concerned, we are dealing with lyric poetry and epigrams. Persian lyric poetry developed a very specific set of conventions, some of which presupposed both a male author and a male addressee, and these conventions were also tacitly present in the epigrammatic forms. The ambiguity of Persian personal pronouns—"he" and "she" are the same word in Persian—means that it is almost never wholly clear which gender is being addressed or talked about in a love poem (ghazal), and it seems likely that many lyric poems by men were addressed to women, but the fallback assumption was that such poems were written by a mature male to an adolescent male; that is, as far as poetic convention indicated, women were wholly excluded from the world of lyric poetry. Again, a Western parallel may help to illustrate what is going on when a woman writes within this traditionally male form.

Early medieval Persian poetry is in many ways similar to the early medieval poetry of southern Europe during the same approximate period—that is, the poetry of the troubadours (this is not the place to go into whether the resemblance was more than a coincidence, given the palpable Arabic proximity to, and apparent influence on, both literatures). The approximate lyric equivalent to the ghazal in troubadour poetry was the canso; female troubadours were called *trobairitz*, and they were, like their female counterparts who wrote in Persian, almost always members of the nobility/aristocracy. The canso was "normally" written by a man to or about a woman, so the particular gender complication (that both poet and addressee were assumed to be male) of the Persian ghazal is absent, but in other respects a female poet writing a canso was in a similar situation to a female Persian poet writing a ghazal. As Linda Paterson has written of the *trobairitz*:

> Conventions are particularly problematic for women composing cansos or love lyrics. The canso form cannot be straightforwardly adapted to a female voice. By placing the woman in a position of dominance, the troubadour canso reverses the gender hierarchy obtaining in real life: the speaking male subject chooses to renounce in fiction the superiority of status he enjoys in fact, as far as gender if not class is concerned. If a woman adopts a submissive position in poetry she conforms to rather than reverses her real situation . . . *

All this is true of women's love poetry in Persian; the added complication that Persian lyric poetry by men is usually assumed to be addressed to a male adolescent does not change the reversal of power dynamics involved, since in a ghazal these male adolescents are conceived of as playing the conventionally female role in a relationship—that is, they are the recipients of admiration, affection, and sexual advances, rather than their initiator. The result is that, when a woman writes a ghazal, she is assuming what is traditionally a man's role; however, as that fictive man she renounces the culturally expected role of male dominance and assumes the woman's role of supplication and inferiority;

---

*Linda M. Paterson, *The World of the Troubadours: Medieval Occitan Society, c.1100–c.1300* (Cambridge, UK: 1993), p. 262.

she is a woman pretending to be a man who pretends to adopt what was traditionally the female role of subservience (we find a somewhat parallel situation in Shakespearean comedy, when boy actors pretended to be women who pretended to be boys). Linda Paterson also writes that "some scholars have identified elements of a female rhetoric in *trobairitz* poetry relating to particularly intense feelings of frustration and deprivation, and a particular concern with real relationships with members of the other sex."[*]

This too seems to be true of certain Persian women poets; even though it is foolhardy to try to extract biographical detail from what are largely conventional poems, love poems by Persian women can often seem more rooted in real circumstances than do the ghazals of many male poets. The vividness and intensity of feeling in some of the love poems of Jahan Malek Khatun (*c.*1324–*c.*1382), for example, can at times seem to indicate something deeper and stronger than the largely conventional emotional gestures to be expected in many ghazals by male poets. The fact that most of the Persian women poets were "amateur" poets (unlike male professional poets, they had no reason to write poems other than their own individual inclination to do so) also suggests that much more personal feeling may be expressed in their lyric poetry than seems to be the case in the poetry of many professional (male) poets.

Before we leave the question of gender, and its ambiguity in love poems by women, it is as well to remember the convention behind the "normative" male ghazal, which is that the poem is, all other things being equal, likely to be about a same-sex relationship, imaginary or real. By the same token, there is nothing to prevent a woman's ghazals from also being about a same-sex

---

[*]Paterson, *The World of the Troubadours*, p. 262.

relationship, and given the relatively restricted social life of most Persian-speaking women in the pre-modern period, it seems more than possible that some if not many of the love poems collected in this anthology were written not only *by* women but also *to* women (as Sunil Sharma has pointed out,* one obvious candidate is the little poem addressed to "Arezu"—an exclusively female name—by the fifteenth-century poet Zaifi Samarqandi, on p. 50).†

The most prolific women poets writing in Persian during the period before 1500, or at least those from whom most poems have survived, are Mahsati (*c.*1089–1159), Jahan Khatun (*c.*1324–*c.*1382), and Mehri (fourteenth/fifteenth century). It is significant that all three of these women were associated with courts whose rulers were descended from central Asian conquerors who had either adopted Islam relatively recently, or only adopted it once they had settled in Iran. Between the eleventh and fifteenth centuries, Iran was overrun first by the Seljuk Turks, then the Mongols under Genghis Khan, and then

---

* Sunil Sharma, "From A'esha to Nur Jahan: The Shaping of a Classical Persian Poetic Canon of Women," *Journal of Persianate Studies* 2 (2002), p. 157.
† Gender is conceived of as extremely fluid in pre-modern Persian poetry, with the same epithets being used to describe both beautiful girls and beautiful boys; the physical ideal implied by descriptions of the beloved in a ghazal is androgynous—a very boyish girl or a very girlish boy. A striking example of this is that in one poem (ghazal 321 in Khanlari's edition [Tehran: 1359/1980], vol. 1, p. 658) Hafez begins by describing the subject of the poem as being "an angel-like houri," and houris are of course conceived of as female; later in the same poem he remarks on the "black line" of the beloved's incipient mustache, who is now clearly being depicted as an adolescent boy.

the Timurids under Timur the Lame (Tamburlaine). All of these peoples were originally nomadic tribes who descended on Iran from the steppes of central Asia, and for the first generations of their rule in Iran they retained much of their central Asian nomadic culture. Gender roles in nomadic cultures tend to be much less strongly demarcated than in sedentary cultures, and women's participation in many aspects of public life is taken for granted in ways that would seem scandalous in traditional sedentary cultures; when the rulers were of nomadic descent, this was true even in Islamic courts, at which we might have expected the women to be secluded from public life as was then the case in much of the rest of the Islamic world. Nomadic peoples did not balk at being ruled by women, and in the Seljuk era (1037–1157) a number of women actively participated in politics, while Mongol women were involved in virtually all aspects of public life, including religious, economic, and military activities. In particular, the Mongols were used to women wielding political power, and at various times in the thirteenth century the Iranian provinces of Kerman and Fars were both ruled by Mongol princesses. Even when female rule was not so unambiguous, the Mongols often married their daughters to members of the local nobility, and in these mixed marriages the Mongol wife tended to have at least as much authority as her native-born husband, if not more. Although it had begun to diminish somewhat, this tradition of relative gender equality, at least at the upper levels of society, continued under the Timurids (mid fourteenth to late fifteenth century).

Given the openness of these dynasties to women's participation in court life, it is unsurprising that Mahsati was said to have sought and gained employment as a scribe at the court of the Seljuk king Sanjar (r. 1118–57), that Jahan Khatun, an Inju princess descended from a mixed Mongol-Persian marriage, became well known as a poet in her own lifetime, or that the poet Mehri was an intimate of the Timurid empress Gowhar Shad (who was seen as a virtual co-ruler while her husband was alive and became the empire's sole ruler after his death in 1447). That the women of the Inju court routinely went unveiled was a mark of their relative social freedom, as was noted by the fourteenth-century traveler Ibn Battuta, who also recounts a revealing anecdote concerning a member of Jahan Khatun's family. During a palace coup one of Jahan's female relatives (the mother of Jahan Khatun's uncle, Abu Es'haq) had been seized by her enemies and was being taken through the bazaar; she tore off the veil in which she had been shrouded by her captors, and appealed for help from the local populace, who immediately recognized her, rallied to her defense, and killed the men who were attempting to abduct her. The fact that she was identified so quickly and so easily indicates that not only did this woman appear at court unveiled, but that she also appeared unveiled in such mundane and potentially disreputable surroundings as the public bazaar. The relative freedom and more or less gender equality of at least aristocratic women in Mongol society was paralleled by the Mongols' religious tolerance, at least during the first century or so of their conquests; historically they were shamanists, but by the time they embarked on their conquest of Asia many were either Christians (especially women for some reason), Moslems, or Buddhists. The Mongol Great Khans enjoyed having the scholars of different religions debate with one another about the true faith,* and the thirteenth-century

---

*The Great Khan Möngke (r. 1251–59), a grandson of Genghis Khan, is said to have remarked to a French envoy: "It is proper to keep the commandments of God. But the Jews say they have received these commandments from Moses, the Arabs say they have them from

historian Matthew Paris recorded that when a Mongol ambassador reached the court of England's King Edward I in 1287, what most surprised and shocked him was that only one religion was allowed there, even though he himself was a Christian and it was his religion that was the favored one.*

From 1500 to the 1800s

Iranian society underwent a radical transformation at the beginning of the sixteenth century, when at the age of fourteen the Safavid ruler Shah Esmail I (r. 1501–24) established his court in Azerbaijan (northwest Iran), declared himself Iran's king, and set about conquering the country to ensure its loyalty. From the Arab conquest onward, Iran had been a very varied nation, with different kings and dynasties ruling in different places, often simultaneously, and with various religious affiliations (predominantly Sunni Moslem but also Shia, with pockets of Christianity, Judaism, and Zoroastrianism scattered about the country, and with a number of Sufi orders that had flourished especially vigorously during the period of Mongol rule). Esmail was a Twelver Shia and he declared Iran to be a Shia country; not only did he insist on political suzerainty, uniting the whole country into

---

Mohammad, and the Christians from Jesus. And there are perhaps other nations that honor their prophets, through whose hands they assert they have received the divine precepts. Therefore how shall we arrive at concord?" Nicholas of Cusa (1401–64), quoted in Jack Weatherford, *Genghis Khan and the Making of the Modern World* (New York: 2004), p. 239. Writing in the early fourteenth century, Marco Polo puts a virtually identical sentence into the mouth of the thirteenth-century Mongol emperor Kublai Khan. Marco Polo, *Travels* (London: 1908, reprinted 1954), p. 159.

*Weatherford, *Genghis Khan*, p. 219.

one political entity under his own rule, but also on religious conformity. Almost overnight, from having been something of a religious hodge-podge with a rather laissez-faire attitude toward private belief, Iran became, nominally and in public at least, a Shia country. Although Sunnism survived in many places, it was relegated to a state of relative political powerlessness and Sunnis were frequently persecuted. The Safavid family, to which Esmail belonged, were members of a Sufi order, and one might have expected Esmail to have had a tolerant attitude toward other Sufi orders than his own, but in reality he saw them as possibly subversive rivals and did his best to eradicate them.

The cultural variety of pre-Safavid Iran, with its concomitant regional differences of government, tradition, and belief, was replaced by a would-be monolithic state that insisted on religious uniformity in so far as this was achievable. Esmail fancied himself as a poet, and in his poetry he claimed semi-divine status, implying that his rule was divinely sanctioned, so that political rebellion became equivalent to religious blasphemy. Esmail's successor, Tahmasp I (r. 1524–76), advised his court poets to occupy themselves with writing poems in praise of the most revered figures of Shia Islam, and the exuberance and diversity of secular Persian poetry found little encouragement at the Safavid court; as courtiers tend to imitate their prince, the patronage of secular poetry by the rich and powerful declined precipitously.

The relative freedom that at least aristocratic women had enjoyed at a number of the courts of pre-Safavid Iran also disappeared. At the court and in the cities the only unveiled women were entertainers, musicians, and courtesans; respectable women lived in seclusion from the world of men. A further curtailing of women's agency is shown by the way in which, with their retreat from the public sphere, fewer women were now taught to read and write, and in seriously religious families illiteracy became the expected norm, even for well-born women. Some Shia clerics were still fulminating against the pernicious evils attendant on women's literacy well into the early twentieth century.

It seems almost inevitable then that there is little evidence of women poets writing in Persian in the heartland of Iran during the Safavid period (1501–1736); with a few exceptions it is only toward the end of the eighteenth century that we begin once again to come across poems by Iranian women poets in any substantial number. And when we read the few poems that were written by women in Iran during this period, we encounter none of the witty high spirits, bawdiness, and flirtatious frivolity that we find in poems by, for example, Mahsati or Mehri or many of their female contemporaries. Instead the predominant tone is proper, serious, unexceptionable.

But while the Safavids were setting up a dynasty in Iran, the Moghuls were establishing theirs in northern India. The Moghul court was rich, Sunni, and, under most of its emperors, relatively tolerant of religious differences. Above all, in the eyes of Iranian poets, it was Persian-speaking,* and during the Safavid period many Iranian poets who had found such slim pickings at home

---

* "Nor let it seem strange that in India, in the countries of the Moghol, the Persian tongue is us'd more perhaps than the Indian itself, since the Mogholian Princes being originally Tartars, and of Samarkand, where the Persian is the natural tongue of the country, have therefore been willing to retain their natural speech in India; in brief, the Persian is the language of the Moghol's court, most spoken and us'd in all publick writings." Pietro della Valle (1586–1652), quoted in Sunil Sharma, *Mughal Arcadia: Persian Literature in an Indian Court* (Cambridge, MA: 2017), p. 3.

flocked* to India to try their fortunes there. As one such émigré poet (Ashraf Mazandarani) put it:

> In Iran there's no market for knowledge
> Even though there's a lot of it for sale;
> In India fame comes to those with skill—
> In the night the brightness of a lamp is visible.

Persian culture had been present in much of northern India before the appearance of the Moghuls; the first Moslem incursions occurred in the early eleventh century, and continued Moslem expansion culminated in the establishment, in 1206, of the Delhi sultanate, which ruled over much of northern India until 1526. The conquerors in this period were mainly of Turkic origin, but among Moslems during the medieval period Persian culture was seen in western and southern Asia as a civilizational ideal (much as French culture was seen in Europe in the eighteenth century), so that Persian mores and the Persian language permeated Moslem rule in India from its inception. It was during this period, for example, that Urdu, a Persianized form of Hindi, emerged as the lingua franca of the area. The establishment of the highly Persianized culture of the Moghul empire, by the first Moghul emperor, Babur, in 1526, was therefore building on what had become by this time a centuries-old philo-Persian foundation. When Babur's son Humayun lost power for a while, it was natural that he should turn to Iran for help, and the Safavid court welcomed him until he was able, with Safavid

---

* "Flocked" is not an exaggeration: an anthology confined to poets who were born in Iran but worked in the Indian Moghul empire between 1500 and 1796—Ahmad Gulchin Ma'ani, *Karavan-e Hend* (Mashhad: 1990)—lists over 1,500 poets, and quotes verses by most of them.

assistance, to regain his throne in 1555. But despite this cultural proximity, the two empires were beginning to diverge in their general ethos; as Safavid Iran became politically and religiously more monolithic and isolationist (as a Shia country in a predominantly Sunni part of the world), Moghul India was entering into a particularly complex relationship with its host country. The emperor Akbar (r. 1556–1605), for example, extended the empire by conquest but also abolished the tax on non-Moslems that was customary in Moslem-ruled countries, and under the influence of Sufi teachers first espoused a form of Islam that attempted to transcend sectarian differences within the faith (his mother was a Persian princess, and both Shia and Sunni were welcome at his court), and then elaborated his own even more inclusive religion (the *din-e elahi,* or divine faith) with the intention of reconciling Hindu and Moslem beliefs. His descendant Prince Dara Shukoh (1615–59) went even further, translating the *Upanishads* into Persian (or so it is claimed, although it seems likely that he commissioned the translation rather than doing it himself, as this would have been an enormous undertaking to manage single-handedly, in terms both of the scholarly knowledge and the time required),* again with the intention of finding common ground between the faiths.

This relatively open and latitudinarian attitude extended to the position of women at the Moghul court. It was only with the accession of Akbar that the institution of the harem was introduced, and it's clear that royal princesses and consorts of the emperor usually enjoyed a kind of freedom that was in many

---

* It is this translation that was translated into Latin by Abraham Hyacinthe Anquetil-Duperron in the late eighteenth century, the version that was used by both Hegel and Schopenhauer, and so became known throughout nineteenth-century Europe.

ways similar to that which had been enjoyed in Iran by women of the court under Mongol rule. If the women of the Moghul court were in theory secluded, this usually did not prevent them from appearing at court functions and festivities, and some of them—for example, Golbadan Beigum, Nur Jahan, and Zib al-Nissa—becoming a byword in the general culture in a way that would by this time have been thought shameful in Iran (the names and characters of a number of imperial consorts and princesses at the Moghul court have become part of the general lore of the Moghul empire; by contrast, although they were often important in squabbles over the royal succession, few female members of the Safavid court have left much trace behind them or are known to any but specialists in Safavid history).*

It is also obvious that many women of the Moghul court were literate, and not merely in the technical sense that they could read and write in a basic fashion, but as accomplished and respected authors. For example, Golbadan, one of Babur's daughters, wrote a biography of her brother Homayun (the *Homayun-nameh*), while her sister Golchehreh's talent was for witty poetry. The best-known such poet was Nur Jahan (1577–1645), the favorite wife of the emperor Jahangir (r. 1605–27); she was a widow aged thirty-four when Jahangir fell in love with her (and this was certainly a love-match since there would have been no other reason for an emperor to marry someone middle-aged, as she would have been considered at this time,

---

*One important exception is the daughter of Shah Tahmasp, Pari Khan Khanom (1548–78), who was known as a poet, although only one poem attributed to her with any certainty has come down to us (see p. 55). She was ambitious and powerful, and for a short time after her father's death was de facto ruler of Iran; at the age of twenty-nine she was murdered at the instigation of a political rival.

and a widow to boot). She had been born in Qandahar, in Afghanistan, to Persian parents who were on their way east as members of the steady stream of Iranians emigrating to India at this time. Her poetry has a distinctive individuality, one that is quite independent, even acerbic at times, but also self-possessed and gently playful. Virtually all pre-modern Persian poetry was written under a pseudonym, and Nur Jahan was said to have used the name "Makhfi" ("Hidden") as her poetic name. This became a name used by a number of women at the Moghul court, the best known of whom was Zib al-Nissa (1638–1701), the daughter of the emperor Aurangzib (r. 1658–1707), who had her locked up for many years as he disapproved of the man she had become engaged to marry (they never did marry). Her poetry, like Nur Jahan's, has a distinctive character—in Zib al-Nissa's case, both witty and wistful, feisty but with an undertow of sorrow. The often personal nature of Moghul women's poetry seems analogous to the portrait tradition that grew up in Moghul painting. Persian miniature depictions of people at this time represented idealized types (the lover, the warrior, the Sufi, and so on) with no attempt at realistic representation or portrayal; Moghul painting, which derived its technique from Persian miniature painting, quite quickly diverged from its model and became personalized, so that any given picture seemed to be of something (or someone) specific, rather than of the kind of Platonic ideal of a subject that Persian painting still aimed for.

In the eighteenth and early nineteenth century we find two important women poets writing in Persian outside of India, at the outer limits, as it were, of Iran. One was Afghan, and the other Kurdish. Associated with the court of the Afghan king Timur Shah Durrani (r. 1772–93), Aysheh Afghani wrote in a number of genres, including quasi-mystical verse and fairly conventional love poems. Perhaps her most distinctive poem is one that reads as a heartfelt elegy on the death of her son, killed fighting in one of Timur Shah Durrani's wars. The Kurdish poet Mastureh Kurdi lived from 1805 to 1848. She too was mistress of a number of poetic genres, including poems in praise of wine (a traditional form going back to the origins of Persian poetry), poems of unrequited love-longing, and poems of religious regret, but her most distinctive poems are addressed to her husband, either regretting his absence or celebrating his presence, declaring her love to him or describing moments in their shared life. She is one of the very few pre-modern Persian women poets who not only wrote about marriage but did so positively, in a way that leaves the reader with the impression of eavesdropping on a real relationship, one that seems to have been in general mutually congenial but that also involved the ups and downs and difficulties attendant on any marriage.

In the same period, the end of the eighteenth and the beginning of the nineteenth century, we also find again, at last, a major woman poet from the Iranian heartland, the poet Reshheh, who was the daughter of the most famous Persian male poet of the period, Hatef Esfahani (d. *c.*1783). Reshheh's poems are polished and elegant, though it must be admitted that they lack the personal distinctiveness of both Aysheh Afghani's and Mastureh Kurdi's poetry; it is as if Aysheh's and Mastureh's relatively peripheral affiliation with the heartland of Persian culture is what enabled each of them to retain an individual voice within the general confines of Persian poetry's conventions, which they both observe and at times slightly stand aside from.

By the time we get to the beginning of the nineteenth century, Safavid rule is a thing of the increasingly distant past. In 1722 the Safavid capital Esfahan had been taken by an invading Afghan army, and the Safavid dynasty to all intents and purposes came to an end. The disintegration of the country (it was invaded more or less simultaneously by the Afghans, the Russians, and the Ottoman Turks) was halted by the warlord Nader Shah, who not only won back lost Iranian territory but invaded northern India and sacked Delhi. He was assassinated in 1747; for a while southern Iran was ruled wisely and well—at least by the chaotic standards of the time—by Karim Khan Zand and returned to relative prosperity, but on his death in 1779 civil war broke out to be finally ended with the armies of the Qajar family declaring victory in 1794 (when the last ruler of the Zand family was deposed), establishing their court in Tehran, and beginning the dynasty that lasted until the 1920s. The second Qajar monarch, Fath Ali Shah (r. 1797–1834), had a very large number of children (generally calculated as fifty-seven sons and forty-six daughters), and one of the notable features of women's cultural presence in the early nineteenth century is the numerous daughters and other female relatives of Fath Ali who wrote poetry. Many of the women in early nineteenth-century Iran who wrote poetry (of what tends to be a rather tentative one-toe-in-the-water kind) that has survived were connected with the Qajar tribe and/or court. But there are two important exceptions to this rather tepid state of affairs: one is the aforementioned Mastureh Kurdi; and the other is Tahereh, also known as Qorrat al-Ayn (1814–52).

From the 1800s to the Present

The nineteenth century in Iran began with an autocracy that was in many respects indistinguishable from the autocracies of most of the previous centuries, and the fundamental social status of women remained as restricted as it had ever been; indeed, women from rich and powerful families were arguably more restricted than had been the case in some parts of Iran during the thirteenth and fourteenth centuries. The century ended with widespread demands for representative government, and with a gradually increasing participation of women in literary and political movements that went hand in hand with growing demands for women's emancipation and social parity with men. The social and political ferment of the century, which grew ever more urgent and widespread, had a striking effect on the kind of poetry women began to write, and was itself fed by the developing consciousness of women's status as this was reflected in their poetry. Obviously women had always known that they were considered to be, and therefore treated as, subservient to their menfolk; the difference was that they now began to feel that it might, at last, be possible to do something about this.

The woman whose life perhaps best represents the beginning of the radically innovative direction in which women's consciousness began to move in the nineteenth century is the poet Tahereh (or Qorrat al-Ayn). Educated by her father, Tahereh from a young age showed an interest in both theology and poetry, and she set off quite literally in search of spiritual enlightenment. Although she never met him in person, she became a follower of Mirza Ali Mohammad of Shiraz, known as the Bab ("the Gate"), who was in the process of founding a new faith derived from Twelver Shi'ism but including aspects considered heretical by the Shia themselves, one of which was the belief that another Prophet would appear in succession to Mohammad (who is known to all Moslems of whatever sect as the "seal"—or the last—of the Prophets). Tahereh became one of the Bab's chief acolytes and proselytizers and took a prominent part in the Babi Conference of Badasht in 1848, the meeting at which Babism is considered to have irreparably broken away from Islam. Her appearance at the conference caused a scandal as she gave her address to the assembled delegates unveiled. As we have seen, aristocratic women had appeared unveiled in Iran at various times during the Middle Ages, and women of the nomadic tribes that still inhabited large areas of Iran often went unveiled; nevertheless, for an educated woman, and one who claimed proximity to someone considered by the conference's audience to be a revered religious figure, to appear in this state at this time was regarded as both unprecedented and disgraceful, even though the Bab himself later defended her decision. After the formal schism with Islam, the Bab and his followers were persecuted wherever they could be found, and the movement went underground. The Bab himself was captured and executed in 1850. In 1852 an unsuccessful attempt on the life of the monarch, Naser al-Din Shah (r. 1848–96), was blamed on the Babis, and many were killed in retribution, including Tahereh, who was strangled, perhaps on direct orders from the shah himself.

The chief events of Tahereh's life—her personal quest for a spiritual leader, her joining and outspokenly supporting a generally despised and reviled religious movement, and not least the symbolic act of her deliberate unveiling in public—all indicate a fiercely independent and strong-minded woman. In terms of her contribution to women's emerging consciousness of their potential roles in public life, the importance of her unveiling should not be underestimated; it said in effect that, in the same way that for her the Bab's teachings represented an emancipation from the old religious order, so her unveiled appearance in public represented an emancipation from the status of women as being hidden and subservient.

But as a poet she looked back as much as she looked forward. For all the daring of her intellectual and public life, she is an almost wholly traditional poet, writing within the tropes and conventions of medieval and subsequent poetry, in which the speaker is supplicatory (and/or celebratory) vis-à-vis the poem's addressee or subject. She differs from most of her female predecessors in the emphatic no-holds-barred religious ardor that she brings to some of her poems, but the rhetoric of these poems, the driving rhythms and the metaphors of drunkenness and erotic obsession, derives virtually unchanged from medieval religious poetry, especially perhaps that of Rumi (1207–73). It was in the two or three generations that came after Tahereh that the substance and rhetoric of women's poetry began to change, and to reflect more clearly women's evolving consciousness of their status, a psychological and social shift of which Tahereh can be said to have been the main harbinger.

A number of social factors facilitated this change. Literacy was becoming more widespread among the daughters of the wealthy and the as yet relatively small middle class. Various newspapers began publication (almost all of them agitating for political reform, and many of them published outside of Iran, in India or Turkey, and then smuggled into the country); some of these papers welcomed contributions, including poetry, by women. Poetry was quite quickly becoming a more democratic medium, often in the form of political or social satire, with a life of its own outside of both court and Sufi circles. Educated women were beginning to form their own social and intellectual groups, some of which joined in the growing agitation for reform. In the period leading up to the Iranian Constitutional

Revolution of 1905–11,* politically oriented poetry by women began to appear in various publications, many of them more or less clandestine. The main demand of such poems was usually that foreign governments cease their interference in the political and economic life of Iran, as the Iranian government was widely seen, with a great deal of justification, as being incapable of warding off foreign influence, particularly that of the Russians and the British, who had spent much of the nineteenth century jockeying with one another for control of the country.† This was often coupled with two other demands, for representative government, and for the emancipation of women. A number of women's poems

---

*Widespread demand for political reform, including representative government, developed throughout Iran in the late nineteenth century. This finally led to Mozaffar ad-Din Shah Qajar (r. 1896–1907) signing a new constitution in 1906, but he died shortly afterward, and his successor on the Persian throne, Mohammad Ali Shah, abrogated the new constitution and had the parliament building bombarded by a Cossack regiment in 1908. Renewed protests led to a march on Tehran by supporters of the constitution, and Mohammad Ali Shah was forced to abdicate in favor of his son Ahmad Shah Qajar, who re-ratified the constitution in 1909. A long period of turmoil ensued, culminating in the coup of 1921, which marked the end of the Qajar dynasty (although in theory Ahmad Shah continued to rule until 1925). The soldier Reza Khan, who had risen quickly through the ranks after joining the Persian Cossack Brigade at the age of sixteen in 1894, took over the government; he declared himself king in 1925, formally taking the name Reza Shah Pahlavi, and was crowned in 1926.

† This culminated in the Anglo-Russian Entente of 1907, which divided Iran into three separate areas of influence: a northern zone in which Russia could have a relatively free hand economically and politically; a southern zone in which the British were to have the same privileges; and a neutral zone between the two. Iran was not invited to send representatives to the conference that arrived at this agreement, and Iranian resentment of its provisions was naturally emphatic and widespread.

at this time take up an admonitory and even mocking attitude toward Iranian men, implying that they are too pusillanimous to do anything about the dire political situation; the implicit question these poems pose is: What use is your vaunted machismo if women have to rouse you to defend your country? Sometimes there almost seems to be a sexual subtext in the verses, as if they are a nineteenth- or twentieth-century equivalent to the relatively frequent poems by medieval women that mocked old men's sexual deficiencies, implicitly comparing their inadequacy with the angry vitality of their dissatisfied partners.

Some of these political poems openly state that if women were socially equal to men, the country would not be in such dire straits. The demand for female emancipation is often made in comparison with the perceived social position of European women, the implication being that if Iranian women could have the same status as their European counterparts, the country would be much better off all round. How far the women voicing these ideas were familiar with the actual status of women in Europe at this time is perhaps open to doubt. Some of their "information" about Europe may well have come from European novels, particularly those written in French, which were beginning to be translated into Persian* (and some women from richer families were able to read French novels in the original), so there was probably an element of fantasy in the literate Iranian women's view of the status of European women in the late nineteenth/ early twentieth century. Nevertheless, many were quite sure that,

---

*Novels by Alain-René Lesage, Alexandre Dumas, Jules Verne, François Fénelon, and the Comtesse de Ségur, as well as some of Molière's plays, and Voltaire's *L'Histoire de Charles XII*, were all translated into Persian before the period of the Iranian Constitutional Revolution. Translated works by Dumas and Molière were particularly well received.

even if they hadn't got all the details exactly right, most European women had a better chance of leading a personally satisfying and relatively free life than most Iranian women, and their poems say this. And here we come upon a paradox inherent in a number of socially conscious poems by women from this period: while insisting that European countries absent themselves from Iranian economic and political affairs, and be forcibly ejected if necessary, a demand is also being made that Iranian women have a similar social status to that of European women. Europe was seen as both the rapacious foreign exploiter of the country, and as a beckoning symbol of what enlightened gender relations could be in a better world. Of course, Iranian opinion was not alone in simultaneously holding these two views of Europe as being both an exploitative adversary and, in some senses at least, a model for desired reforms.

Two of the most important Persian-language women poets of the past five hundred years dominate the first half of the twentieth century, or at least they do so in retrospect, as the poetry of one of them was almost completely unknown until after her death. The poets in question are Alam Taj (1883–1946), whose pen-name was "Zhaleh" ("Dew"), and Parvin Etesami (1907–41). Alam Taj, who has been called the first feminist poet to have written in Persian, came from a prominent aristocratic family, and her first poems were published when she was still a teenager at the suggestion of the then poet laureate (Malek al-Shoara Bahar), who was a family friend. But she was married off at the age of fifteen to a military man, Ali Morad Khan, who was much older than she was and who had no interest in literature or indeed in any of the arts; if Alam Taj is to be believed, he was also incapable of showing her affection or approval. He forbade her to write,* and though she continued to do so, she wrote secretly and hid her poems in books and drawers and various other places around the house, where they remained until they were discovered, after her death, by her son. She outlived her husband, and it's not wholly clear why she continued to hide her poems after his death; perhaps she had by then despaired of ever having an audience, and the habit of secrecy, developed over so many years, had become too internalized and ingrained to break.

Her poems are intensely personal and in the main intensely unhappy. One of her chief subjects is her loathing—the word doesn't seem too strong—of her husband, but she extrapolates this sense of personal injury into vehement protests against the social norms and customs that had put her into her intolerable marriage in the first place; as she succinctly puts it in one poem, "Woman's crime in our country is to be a woman."† She inveighs against the marrying-off of young women to old men for familial reasons; she argues that women should be men's equals socially, and that intellectually and spiritually they *are* men's equals, if not their superiors; she protests at the subjugation of women by men, and she advises women to burn their veils. In one of her most poignant longer poems, she looks forward to a future, one in which she will not share, when the women of Iran will be equal

---

* This of course seems appalling to us, but before we rush to judgment, we should remember that at this time such husbandly prohibitions were also considered quite normal in the West. For example, Gustav Mahler forbidding his wife Alma to compose any more music once they were married, in 1902, happened four years after Alam Taj's husband forbade her to write any more poetry once they were married, in 1898.

† *Divan-e Alam Taj Qa'em-Maghami, Zhaleh*, ed. Ahmad Karami (Tehran: 1374/1995), p. 149.

citizens in their own country, and more than almost any other poet she sees this change as coming from the West:

> A breeze blows from the land of the living
> Towards this country, making my limbs revive;
> The song of women's freedom comes from the west
> To the east, but my place there will be empty.

The biography of her much better-known contemporary, Parvin, was in its early stages remarkably similar to that of Alam Taj. Both were extremely close to their fathers, who encouraged their writing when they were young; both were first published when they were still adolescents at the instigation of Bahar; both made unhappy marriages with military men who were uninterested in their poetic vocation and who provided them with little or no emotional support. The major difference is that Parvin's poems were published in her own lifetime, and although appreciation of her poetry was grudging at first,* some was enthusiastic (and Iran's foremost literary historian, Zabihollah Safa, was later to call her "the most accomplished of all Iran's women poets"†), whereas Alam Taj's poems remained unknown till after her death; another difference is that Alam Taj's father, who also seems to

---

*Ridiculous as it may seem, a number of articles and even books were written claiming that Parvin's poems could not be by her since they had obviously been written by a man; the main "evidence" for this claim was that the poems had such a sophisticated vocabulary and were so well written that it would be absurd to think that a woman could have written them. This idiotic claptrap was still being repeated in the 1970s, over thirty years after Parvin's death in 1941. Frequently the highest praise that was bestowed on Parvin by writers who accepted that her poems were in fact by her was that she "wrote like a man."
† *Ganj-e Sokhan* (Tehran: n.d.), vol. 3, p. 291.

have been her closest friend, died shortly after her marriage, whereas Parvin's father lived for almost as long as she did. As an adult, Alam Taj was emotionally extremely isolated and she lacked even the satisfaction of knowing that others could read her poems; if Parvin's (very brief) married life was unhappy, at least she experienced the praise and respect of a number of the most important poets of her time, which must have given her some solace, and she didn't lose the love and support of her father until a few years before her death.

The subject matter Parvin constantly returns to is the sufferings of those in the lower reaches of society—ragamuffin children, the working poor and the unemployed poor, the aged who have no one to turn to for help or support—but despite the strong sense of economic and social injustice that permeates her poetry, she has no political agenda, no revolutionary call to arms, and there is no sense in her writings that the despised and rejected should rise up against their oppressors.* Given her social conservatism, it is perhaps not surprising that her technique is strictly traditional and owes a great deal to the widespread history of moralized "advice" poetry in Persian, especially to the didactic verse of the major thirteenth-century poet Sa'di (one foreign influence was that of the seventeenth-century French poet and fabulist Jean de La Fontaine; her affinity for his poetry probably sprang from the fact that La Fontaine's fables were in some ways

---

*For an English-speaking reader, she can seem like a poetic Dickens: that is, one who empathetically records the sufferings of the lowest members of her society (often in terms that can seem to readers untouched by such sufferings to be grossly sentimental), but who, like Dickens, has no remedy to offer other than the generosity and kindness of society's wealthier members. Like Dickens, she is constantly, explicitly or implicitly, admonishing her readers and herself to be kind.

similar to the moralizing anecdotes to be found in traditional Persian poetry). Farzaneh Milani has pointed out that Parvin is one of the very few Persian-language poets who wrote no love lyrics or erotic verse of any kind,* and we can occasionally see in her poems something that is also discernible in some of Alam Taj's poetry, which is a kind of revulsion at female sexuality and female vanity, and to any sort of display that is meant to attract erotic attention. She is not as extreme in her condemnation of what she sees as women's failings as Alam Taj can be (see, for example, the section "Woman" in Alam Taj's poem "Life's Image" on p. 137), but she implies that if women don't want to be considered solely in sexual terms, they should not dress or behave in ways that are likely to provoke unwanted male interest. Both of them emphasize that it is far better for women to be modest and chaste in their demeanor than to be showily attractive, or even particularly noticeable; that is, for all their innovative genius, and their demands for both education and social equality with men, they have internalized their culture's standards of how the ideal woman should behave, and certainly how she should behave in public.

Although their childhoods were spent in literate families that valued their daughters' poetic talents and aspirations, when they became adults Alam Taj and Parvin were each quite isolated as a poet. It's unlikely that Parvin even knew of Alam Taj's existence, and neither of them belonged to a group of like-minded women poets who could provide one another with mutual support, act as a sounding-board for new ideas, or offer friendly but critical advice on their latest verse. For the generation of poets who followed, and who came to define modern Persian poetry by

---

* Farzaneh Milani, *Veils and Words: The Emerging Voices of Iranian Women Writers* (Syracuse, NY: 1992), p. 120.

women as a self-consciously contemporary phenomenon that broke with many of the traditions of the past, the situation was very different. As young women, Simin Behbahani (1927–2014), Lobat Vala (b. 1930), and Forugh Farrokhzad (1934–67) met regularly to discuss poetry and to share their new poems with one another. As Simin Behbahani later wrote:

> We made up a group to which a number of women poets, as well as those interested in poetry, painters and other kinds of artist, were invited and every week we met together. We read our poetry to each other and we discussed poetry and other subjects. At that time we were three poet friends and Dr. Sadraddin Elahi called us "the three musketeers". The three of us went to every literary gathering . . .*

One of the subjects the three discussed was the break with the traditional metrical system that had been initiated by Nima Yushij (1897–1960), who became known as the father of modern Persian poetry. Among Yushij's technical innovations was the popularization of a loosely metrical quatrain in relatively short lines that rhymed *abcb*, and a number of the early poems by the "three musketeers" were written in this form, which became a kind of halfway house to the fully fledged free verse that came increasingly to dominate Persian poetry in the second half of the twentieth century.

Later in the same essay Simin Behbahani describes her two friends as they were when the three of them were young together:

---

* Simin Behbahani's introduction to Lobat Vala's poetry collection *Farda-ye Digar* ("Another Tomorrow") (London: 2008), pp. 12–13.

Lobat was kind, naïve, sweet in her conversation, and magnanimous. She never said anything harsh. She never complained about anyone. She overlooked anything negative and was a very loyal friend . . . Forugh on the other hand, because of being constantly highly-strung, and because of the difficulties in her life, was quarrelsome, reckless and full of expectations.[*]

Forugh was to become easily the most famous of the modern women poets who wrote in Persian, and she is still perhaps the only one whose name is widely known outside of Iran.

Forugh Farrokhzad was born into a military family in 1934, and married at the age of sixteen. She had a son, and after three years of marriage she and her husband were divorced; one of the great sorrows of her life was that her husband's family received custody of the child (as was usual in Iran at this time after a divorce) and she saw him only occasionally for the rest of her life. In 1958 she met the writer and film-maker Ebrahim Golestan and began a relationship with him that lasted until 1967 when she was killed in a car crash. Forugh's eager hypersensitivity to experience, which often seems to find itself rebuffed by the world, is everywhere evident in her poetry, which can be read as a kind of psychological collodion plate responsive to every shade of light and dark that flits before it. Her "highly-strung" psychological state, as Simin Behbahani characterized it, together with her extreme sensitivity to the difficult vicissitudes of her life, had its cost in serious bouts of depression, and at least one almost-successful suicide attempt.

---

[*] Behbahani, introduction to Vala, *Farda-ye Digar*, p. 13.

Taken together, the titles of the four books of poems she published in her lifetime spell out the trajectory of her life as she herself saw it: *The Captive*, *The Wall*, *Rebellion*, and *Another Birth*.*
The most famous, and at the time of publication scandalous, aspect of her poetry was its acknowledgment and celebration of female desire and sexual pleasure, whether or not—and it seems from her poems preferably not—this occurs within the confines of marriage. That she should discuss female sexuality at all in her poetry in Iran at that time was remarkable, and it is perhaps not surprising that hers is, at least in her early poems, a relatively fraught celebration of the subject. If we compare her poems that deal with sexuality with poems on the same subject by medieval women writing in Persian, we see a major difference. The insouciant bawdiness of a fourteenth-/fifteenth-century poet such as Mehri is predicated on finding sex available, normal, and funny; much of the sensuality of Forugh Farrozkhzad's poetry is predicated on notions of sin, the flouting of socially acceptable gender roles, and transgression. The subject is charged with tension, anxiety, and defiance, and there are few purely lighthearted moments. Sexual pleasure is equated with—or at least inextricably linked with—sin, even as the notion of sex as sin is denied, and it is no coincidence that what is perhaps her best-known poem about sex is called, exactly, "Sin" (see p. 182). The title can be read as ironic (the poet is saying that sexual pleasure outside of marriage is not a sin, whatever society may think) but "sin" still provides the context and ethos within which the subject is seen, and the possibility of sexual pleasure is linked to notions of transgression.

---

* *The Captive* (1334/1955), *The Wall* (1335/1956), *Rebellion* (1337/1958), *Another Birth* (1343/1964). A fifth book, *Let Us Believe in the Dawn of a Cold Season*, appeared posthumously (1353/1974).

Forugh Farrokhzad has often been compared to Sylvia Plath,* a comparison that is valid, both in reference to their poetry and to the ways in which their work and more especially their lives have been mythologized since their deaths. Both poets can adopt a rather apocalyptic tone, especially when dealing with notions of patriarchy and masculinity; both write from deep within their own psyches and their own psychological preoccupations, so that their poems can sometimes seem to sweat with irresolvable anxiety or nausea. The lives of both poets, their unhappy marriages, their violent deaths, their often expressed wish somehow to transcend or escape from the circumstances in which they found themselves, have become iconic for a number of later women poets in their respective cultures, almost as though they constitute a kind of irresistible archetype of what it means to be a woman poet in the contemporary world.

The poet whom Simin Behbahani described as "kind, naïve, sweet in her conversation, and magnanimous," Lobat Vala, is perhaps the most conservative of the three, both technically and in her choice of subjects and her expressed attitudes toward them. Much of her poetry had, and continues to have, a direct appeal that reached a much wider audience than was usual for contemporary verse, and a number of her poems were used as the lyrics of popular songs. About sexuality she is usually very modest (see, for example, her poem "Footprint" on p. 174), and Behbahani's description of her personality is also applicable to many of her poems. She lived far longer than Farrokhzad (at the time of writing, she is still alive), long enough to experience both political and personal disillusion, and her later poems can

---

*For an informative, in-depth comparison between Forugh Farrokhzad and Sylvia Plath, see Leila Rahimi Bahmany's *Mirrors of Emancipation and Entrapment: Forugh Farrokhzad and Sylvia Plath* (Leiden: 2015).

sometimes have a bitter tang to them that is largely absent from her earlier work.

Simin Behbahani herself died in 2014 at the age of eighty-seven. Her range is very wide, and includes personal love poems, poems of social anger and political commentary, poems of self-questioning introspection, and a number of moving vignettes of suffering (particularly the suffering of exploited and disadvantaged women). A reader of her work has a sense of someone whose whole life has been given to poetry and to the fight for social and political justice. To compare her to a non-Iranian writer, we have to reach for the names of similarly inclusive and compassionate authors who can rise to any technical challenge as if it were no challenge at all; perhaps the non-Iranian poet she most resembles, in the breadth of her sympathies, her steadfast personal and political integrity, and her mastery of formal possibilities, is Pablo Neruda.

When Simin Behbahani wrote about the "three musketeers," she also referred to another poet friend, Zhaleh Esfahani (1921–2007), who occasionally attended their meetings. Zhaleh Esfahani, like many writers of her generation in many parts of the world, responded positively to the siren call of communism, and quite early in her life became involved in leftist literary and political circles. In 1946 she married a prominent member of the Iranian communist party (Hezb-e Tudeh), and in 1947 she left Iran for the Soviet Union. She studied in Moscow, where she wrote a PhD dissertation on Malek al-Shoara Bahar, the poet laureate who had helped both Alam Taj and Parvin Etesami publish their adolescent poems. She stayed in the Soviet Union for over thirty years, until the Islamic Revolution of 1979, when she briefly returned to Iran (see her poem "Return" on p. 161). However, she soon became disillusioned with the course the Revolution was taking, and left Iran for London, where she lived until her death.

Her poetry is strongly marked by her political sympathies, and in retrospect much of it can seem naïvely gullible about the promise of communism, but in this she is no different from many poets of her generation in many parts of the world, and her verse shows that she had a genuine lyric gift which never left her even in her most ideologically committed poems.

Zhaleh Esfahani, Lobat Vala, and Simin Behbahani all lived well into their eighties. All three poets were extraordinarily persistent and still occupied themselves in writing poems of hope at the end of their lives, never quite giving up the idealism of their youth. Whatever one thinks of their poetry in aesthetic terms, their sheer tenacity—to life, to their ideals, to their calling as poets—surely commands our admiration. To look at their achievements over such long lives, and often in such extremely difficult circumstances, brings to mind Edgar's reverent valedictory words at the end of *King Lear*: "The oldest hath borne most; we that are young / Shall never see so much, nor live so long."

For a while the Islamic Revolution of 1979 seemed as though it would be as transformative of Iranian society as the Safavid revolution of 1501 had been, and in some ways this has proved to be the case. The gradual secularization of Iranian society that had been going on since the 1920s was halted and in so far as was possible reversed, and women in particular bore the brunt of this reversal. In 1936 the ruler at the time, Reza Shah, had banned the veil and headscarf, and the edict was forcefully implemented; his son, Mohammad Reza Shah (r. 1941–79), did not withdraw the edict but neither did he vigorously enforce it, and whether a woman veiled herself or not became more or less a question of personal choice. With the Islamic Revolution the veil became mandatory; some aspects of male dress (for example, the wearing of ties, which was seen as Western and therefore reprehensible) were also proscribed, and how a person dressed became a matter of political acquiescence or protest, with skirmishes between "guardians of public morality" and members of the public becoming a common occurrence. The dress codes have been relaxed at times and then tightened again, depending on which faction of the clerical government has the upper hand, and how much hair a woman was able to display uncovered by her veil became for many a daily preoccupation.

Of course the concern with how people dressed in public was only an outward symbol of a much deeper rethinking of gender roles throughout society, but there was no question of women being pushed back into a solely private and silent existence. Much of the female population of the country was now literate, and large numbers of middle-class women had gone on to undergraduate and graduate education; more women have been enrolled at Iranian universities than men for most years since the Revolution, outnumbering men by three to two in the 2012 entrance exams, and at one point the government became so concerned that women were becoming a major part of the country's educated élite that many university courses were declared to be open to male students only. It seemed that a century of women's activism, from the first stirrings of political consciousness expressed in the verse of such poets as Shahin Farahani, Jannat, Kasma'i, and Nimtaj, from the late nineteenth century until the present, would go for naught.

Many partially or completely secularized families emigrated, with the result that there is a large diaspora of educated Iranians in most countries of the Western world. When families as a whole did not emigrate, their educated daughters often did. But many professional women, torn between patriotism and irritation at the structures imposed by the theocratic government, stayed in Iran; some, like the lawyer Shirin Ebadi, who was awarded the 2003 Nobel Peace Prize, have worked openly and tirelessly to promote the rights of women, while others have formed a kind of unofficial semi-underground intellectual opposition. One result of a large number of educated women feeling that their freedom was unnecessarily curtailed and their intellectual gifts largely discounted has been a veritable explosion of women's writing in both prose and verse. Many and perhaps most of the best-known Iranian novelists to have emerged in the forty years since the Revolution are women, and in the same period very large numbers of women have published books of poetry. Much of it is not even implicitly in opposition to the values of the Islamic Revolution, but some of it is, and the more outspoken poets have either fled the country after clashing with the authorities, or done so as a precautionary measure.

It is the outspoken poets of course who have become best known, if often only among their fellow exiles, but there have been important women poets who have been supportive of the Revolution; the most significant of these is Tahereh Saffarzadeh (1936–2008), favored by Ayatollah Khomeini and highly praised by his successor, Ayatollah Khamenei. To a Western observer she can seem a paradoxical figure: unlike many poets who have supported the Revolution, she wrote in free verse rather than in the "classical" metrical system of pre-modern Persian verse; she gained an MA in creative writing and cinematography from the University of Iowa, but her poetry rarely seems deracinated in the way that verse by other Iranian poets who studied in the

West can sometimes appear to be;* her Islamic faith was central to her sense of herself, and as well as poetry she wrote extensively on the Qor'an, but unlike many Moslem traditionalists she was also someone whose poetry insists on the central validity and importance of women's experience, and their parity with men.

Saffarzadeh's poetry is in the main direct and clearly comprehensible, and this is in sharp contrast to the poetry of some Iranian women writers who find themselves at odds with the values and practices of the Revolution, whose poetry is often cryptic, surreal, and oblique in ways that can recall the poetry of some Eastern European poets before the fall of the Soviet Union, and presumably for the same reasons. Such poems convey a sense of pervasive illogicality, dystopia, and anxiety because this is seen as the soul's almost inevitable condition in such surroundings, and also because a more unambiguous statement of discontent might well provoke censorship and state retaliation. The practice has created a distinctive and recognizable poetic dialect, one that has become widely admired and adopted in dissident and consciously avant-garde circles, some members of which see obscurity as a badge of honor and the relative clarity of much of Saffarzadeh's poetry as indicating, at best, both political and aesthetic naïveté.

---

*She studied in Iowa while Mohammad Reza Pahlavi was shah of Iran, at a time when he was largely seen by self-consciously progressive intellectuals in Iran as a Western puppet. She later said in an interview that while she was in Iowa she felt closest to the leftist South American poets studying there, poets who in many cases, like Saffarzadeh herself, saw the United States as at least partially responsible for political repression in their home countries, and this may well have had some effect on her future political allegiances.

Tahereh Saffarzadeh received what was in effect almost a state funeral,* and the then president Mahmud Ahmadinejad delivered a eulogy in her praise. But when Simin Daneshvar (the first Iranian woman novelist, and one of the most significant) died in 2012, and the major poet Simin Behbahani died in 2014, the state took virtually no notice of their deaths, and this indicates the extent to which the evaluation of artistic worth has become severely politicized. Ayatollah Khomeini was on record as admiring the poetry of Parvin Etesami, and so her poetry tends to be discounted by many who are opposed to the Islamic Revolution, even though she died long before it happened (and given her concern for women's social and political emancipation—as expressed, for example, in her poem beginning "Once women in Iran . . ." on p. 146—it's doubtful that she would have thought very highly of the Ayatollah); Simin Behbahani espoused largely secular values in her poetry, and so supporters of the Revolution tend to disparage or ignore her work.

Selecting the Poems in this Volume

It is not a difficult task to select women poets from the pre-modern period for inclusion in an anthology like this one: from almost every century the anthologist's task has already been largely completed over time, and he or she can only "select"

---

*Auden has succinctly summed up the relationship between politically acceptable poetry and contemporary autocracies: " . . . the poetry he invented was easy to understand . . . / When he laughed, respectable senators burst with laughter / And when he cried the little children died in the streets." "Epitaph on a Tyrant," W. H. Auden, *Collected Poems* (New York: 1976), p. 183.

among the few survivors; this would be as true for most European languages as it is for Persian. For the earlier centuries covered by this book, a high proportion of what is available is, necessarily, included here; for the present century only a very small proportion of what is available is, equally necessarily, included. Furthermore, as time has not yet begun its winnowing process on the work of contemporary poets, choosing whose work is likely to continue to be valued is at best something of a guessing game.

In her book-length poem *Aurora Leigh*, which, to expand slightly on Wordsworth's subtitle to *The Prelude*, might be called "The Growth of a Woman Poet's Mind," Elizabeth Barrett Browning incidentally provides a metaphor for the difficulty of assessing the art and artists of one's own time:

> We'll suppose
> Mount Athos carved, as Persian Xerxes schemed,
> To some colossal statue of a man.
> The peasants, gathering brushwood in his ear,
> Had guessed as little as the browsing goats
> Of form or feature of humanity
> Up there,—in fact, had travelled five miles off
> Or ere the giant image broke on them . . .
>   . . . 'Tis even thus
> With times we live in . . .*

That we lack sufficient perspective on our own times to judge them with any but myopic eyes is borne out by many earlier anthologies that seem fine until they reach their compilers' contemporaries. When W. B. Yeats made his selection of poets for

---

*Elizabeth Barrett Browning, *Aurora Leigh* (London: 1857), p. 188.

his *Oxford Book of Modern Verse 1892–1935*, published in 1936, he chose a group of names that almost no lay reader or literary historian would now come up with. Yeats's starting point was the death of Tennyson in 1892, and he included over ninety poets, a good half of whom have by now been almost completely forgotten by all but the most assiduous literary specialists in the period. He also excluded a number of poets that any modern anthologist would certainly include (for example, the poets of the First World War—Owen, Gurney, and Rosenberg—and although he included three Indian poets who wrote in English, the only Americans to have made the grade are those who were living or had lived in England; and even from that small number Robert Frost is absent). My point is obvious: it is very unlikely that subsequent generations will wholeheartedly agree with the selection of poetry by an earlier anthologist from the work of his or her contemporaries, and where Yeats failed it is at least equally likely that my guesses as to who and what will seem interesting in the future will be no better than his were.

Poetry of the past is best known to scholars; poetry of the present becomes known to scholars, but it is best known to the poets themselves and hence, because the field is so wide, for verse by living poets I have solicited the recommendations and advice of friends, poets, and scholars who are familiar with contemporary Persian poetry. Nevertheless, there may well be a number of modern poets whose work is absent from this volume whom others would have included, and not all of those whose suggestions I have followed would endorse all of this anthology's inclusions. That said, the contemporary poems translated here have earned their place in this anthology by what I believe to be their aesthetic qualities, their representative importance, or the distinctiveness of a given poet's voice, and usually by a combination of all three of these characteristics.

To read through this anthology is to become aware of how a large number of motifs and tropes have continued to exist in women's poetry written in Persian from its inception to the present. But although many persist, many are also transformed over time. For example, pre-modern Persian-language poets, men and women alike, often use the metaphor of the self as a bird that is trapped in a cage (Hafez is particularly fond of this image), and modern women poets also use the same metaphor from time to time. But the meaning has changed: in pre-modern poetry, the metaphor has a spiritual or metaphysical sense, as it refers to the soul trapped within the body while it longs to return to its original freedom in heaven; in contemporary poetry by women, it tends to refer to a woman trapped in an unwanted and resented relationship with a man, usually her husband.

Similarly, the subject of young women being married off to old men is one that we find in Persian poetry written by women in both medieval and contemporary poetry. But the medieval poets and the contemporary poets concentrate on different moments within the relationship, and have a quite different emotional tone. Medieval poets such as Mehri, Zaifi, and Bibi Mah Ofaq refer to the experience of the married woman, who has perhaps been married for some time, and who is complaining about her husband's sexual inadequacy; the tone is contemptuous and mocking, the poems exist to express anger but also to elicit derisive laughter. And we feel that the poems are written primarily for an audience of other women who will know exactly what is being talked about and can join in the joke. Modern poets such as Alam Taj, Forugh Farrokhazad, and Fevzieh Rahgozar Barlas who refer to the same topic tend to concentrate on the moment of the wedding itself, and on the child-bride who is about to enter into a relationship which the poet implies will be cruelly shocking and humiliating for her, and which can hardly be expected to develop into a mutually satisfactory marriage. The tone is one of implied outrage, pity, and horror; there is no question of laughter, derisive or otherwise, and the audience is anyone, male or female, who has a conscience and is capable of sharing the poet's indignation.

A third example of how something that was there from the beginnings of Persian poetry has persisted, and in doing so become something new, is the trope of longing for someone who is absent. This is a very common theme in pre-modern Persian poetry, expressed in words that mean "far away," "separation," "exile," "yearning," part of a vocabulary which has for centuries been devoted to the subject, with the result that these words are redolent with connotations of aching, unfulfilled need. Among the numerous female poets now living in the Persian-speaking diaspora, exactly the same vocabulary, with the same connotations, is used to indicate longing for the place that was once home, for Iran, or for Afghanistan.

I have emphasized in this introduction the importance of poetic conventions in the development of Persian poetry, and the way that these conventions have persisted, sometimes for many centuries. But I hope it goes without saying that the poets represented in this book are much more than skillful deployers of a set of poetic rules dictating the subject matter of a particular genre of poems, and how such poems should be written. Each of the poets here was of course a specific individual with her own experiences who lived in a particular time and place, and if she used poetic convention she did so in a way that ensured that at least some of her poems survived, unlike the vast majority of poems written within the same conventions; if she belonged to a particular time, she was not merely a representative of her time. As the biographer Lytton Strachey observed, "Human beings are too important to be treated as mere symptoms of the past."* The social and poetic constraints within which these poets wrote are the "past" to which Strachey refers; such constraints are real and insistent, omnipresent even, and are the chief context within which this poetry was written. But the individuals who wrote the poems are "too important," too distinctive, to be defined solely in this way, and this is obvious when we look at examples from this volume: Mehri's high-spirited irritation with her husband; Makhfi's isolation that is both anguished and flirtatious; Jahan Khatun bewailing her family's loss of power; Aysheh Afghani lamenting her son killed in battle; Tahereh striking out as a new kind of woman in a new religion; Alam Taj foreseeing a better future for the women of Iran; Parvin preoccupied with the privations of the poor . . . and so on.

A further constraint on these women's lives, and on our knowledge of them, is indicated by the fact that history has usually defined them almost entirely in terms of their male relatives; they are the daughter of so and so, or the wife of so and so, or the mother of so and so, and often this is all we know about them. If they come from the lower reaches of society, they may be defined solely by their professions—they are "female singers," or "entertainers," or "courtesans," and frequently we don't even know their names. It is undeniable that almost all of the poets represented in this anthology lived or live in a male-dominated and directed society, and their relative anonymity should come as no surprise; but as anyone who is familiar with Iranian society and history knows, the presence of tough, strong-minded, highly intelligent, and eminently capable women has been a constant in that history. This was perhaps most spectacularly shown in the

---

*Lytton Strachey, *Eminent Victorians* (Harmondsworth, UK: 1977), p. 10.

widespread and very active participation of women in the events surrounding the Constitutional Revolution in the early years of the twentieth century, but it has been a persistent presence from the beginning until the present. The conventions of pre-modern Persian lyric poetry, both male and female, presupposed that the poet wrote in a supplicatory tone to or about the object of his or her attentions, but in women's poetry written within this tradition a strain of defiance, independence, audacity, effrontery, and sheer cheek, is there from the beginning; it rises to a crescendo in the late nineteenth and early twentieth centuries, and resolves into a consciously female-oriented poetics in the mid and late twentieth century.

It will be clear to any reader that while women's poetry in Persian has its own distinguishing characteristics, it also shares many of its themes, moods, and strategies with women's poetry in other languages. Poems of longing for an absent or negligent lover are particularly common among women poets in many cultures, for example: Sulpicia in ancient Rome; Ono no Komachi in ninth-century Japan; Jahan Khatun in fourteenth-century Iran; Louise Labé in sixteenth-century France; Gaspara Stampa in sixteenth-century Italy. We might argue that such poems are common among male poets too, but there is a difference, in that social constraint has almost always been much more inhibiting in the case of a woman, who for much of human history has been powerless in ways that do not affect a male lover. He has his beloved's indifference to complain about; she has her beloved's indifference *and* her relative social helplessness, which compounds this, to be concerned about. There is a sense that if worse comes to worst, a man can go off and find someone else, but the socially curtailed life of a woman writing such a poem meant that such choices were unlikely to be available to her, so that, especially in the throes of erotic obsession, her situation can present itself as much more desperate than that of the male lover.

Common to many women poets is a sense of being socially constrained not to act as erotic desire dictates (women have to be sexually modest), all the while experiencing an overwhelming need to do so: the Roman poet Sulpicia, for example, says in one poem that she hates conforming to convention and putting on a public face, yet we know she does this because in another poem she tells us that she regrets nothing more than that "I left you alone last night, wanting to hide the ardor I felt."* Similarly, the erotic isolation of the French poet Louise Labé, and the need to "live discreetly," torments her:

> I am always unhappy, living discreetly,
> and I can find no contentment
> if I do not sometimes make some kind of foray out of
>   myself.†

Parallels to Sulpicia's and Louise Labé's complaints are not hard to find in pre-modern Persian poems written by women. Sometimes tropes used by women poets turn up in more than one culture: the poet's thoughts being as "tangled" as her hair on the morning after a lover has left is a metaphor that appears in both Persian and Japanese poetry by women, for example. The contempt expressed by the fourteenth-/fifteenth-century Persian poet Mehri for her husband's impotence finds a coincidental echo in the words of the sixteenth-century Chinese woman poet Huang O:

---

* "Hesterna quam te solum quod nocte reliqui, / ardorem cupiens dissimulare meum."
† "Toujours suis mal, vivant discrètement, / Et ne me puis donner contentement / Si hors de moi ne fais quelque saillie."

You've made me all wet and slippery
but no matter how hard you try
nothing happens.*

And the poem by an unnamed Persian female entertainer lamenting that those she likes aren't interested in her while those she doesn't like are (see p.15) finds a parallel in the words of a Japanese geisha, also unnamed:

When it's the man I love
he goes by and doesn't come in
but men I hate—
a hundred times a day.†

One of the most noticeable similarities in pre-modern women's poetry is how in many cultures women poets have come from society's extremes in terms of their wealth and social prestige; they were either members of royal or aristocratic families, or paid entertainers and women of the town available for hire: courtiers or courtesans, princesses or prostitutes.

The major uniting factors in much women's poetry from the twentieth and twenty-first centuries have been the struggle for women's emancipation and the specifics of a woman's, as opposed to a man's, life. It is also true that many women poets over the past fifty years or so have turned their backs on the whole notion of "women's poetry," seeing it as a covertly demeaning category, and

---

* *Women Poets of China*, trans. Kenneth Rexroth and Ling Chung (New York: 1972), p. 61.
† *Women Poets of Japan*, trans. Kenneth Rexroth and Ikuko Atsumi (New York: 1977), p. 137.

insisting that their verse be read simply as poetry, outside of any considerations of the poet's gender. However, it is also true that, for much of the pre-modern period, women in general, and certainly women in Persian-speaking countries, tended to have quite separate life-experiences from those of most men in the societies in which they lived, and that the limits of these experiences were prescribed largely by men rather than by women themselves. The specifics of their lives were in many ways different from those of men's lives, and these specifics were in at least some sense not of their own choosing. Different lives, with a different sense of what is allowed and who is doing the allowing, produce different types of literature, and it therefore seems legitimate to consider women's literature, and so women's poetry, as a distinct category. While it is obviously one that overlaps very largely with that of poetry by men, it has nevertheless its own specifics and centers of interest that are sometimes separate from those of men's poetry. That women's poetry often echoes the values and presuppositions of men's poetry, even when these seem to run counter to women's own interests, can easily be accounted for: as Joanna Woods-Marsden has written, in discussing the "masculinist ideology" of some paintings by the sixteenth-century Italian female artist Sofonisba Anguissola: "Although the ideology is transparently patriarchal to the twentieth century, it would surely not have been seen in these terms by an individual living at the time. Ideology veils overt power relations by making them seem part of natural law to all, including those victimized by it."*

---

*Joanna Woods-Marsden, *Renaissance Self-Portraiture* (New Haven and London: 1998), p. 209. Part IV (pp. 185–222) of Woods-Marsden's book deals with women painters in Renaissance Europe; the whole section provides a fascinating insight into women working in a parallel artistic field to that of women poets within what was a traditionally and predominantly male artistic environment.

Translator's Note

It is a great privilege to work as a scholar, in however humble a capacity, in the field of a poetry that is not written in one's own first language, and to try to produce adequate translations of that poetry. I am very sensible of this, as I am of the responsibility of offering such translations to a wider audience, especially, in the case of this book, as only a few of these poems, particularly the pre-modern ones, have been translated before, certainly into English or even, to the best of my knowledge, into any language. Each language has of course its own specificity, tone, atmosphere, "weight"—something that is usually very difficult to define but which becomes more and more palpable the longer someone who is not a native speaker studies the language and lives with it. In translating these poems, I have frequently found myself thinking of a quatrain by the great Argentinian poet Jorge Luis Borges, given here in Alastair Reid's beautiful translation:

> You will never recapture what the Persian
> Said in his language woven with birds and roses,
> When, in the sunset, before the light disperses,
> You wish to give words to unforgettable things.*

---

* "No volverá tu voz a lo que el persa / Dijo en su lengua de aves y de rosas, / Cuando al ocaso, ante la luz dispersa, / Quieras decir inolvidables cosas."

A Note on the Sources

For poets of the twentieth and twenty-first centuries I have mostly translated from published collections of their works and, in the case of some contemporary poets, from websites that include their poems. The poetry of a small number of women poets writing in Persian before the twentieth century (such as Jahan Khatun and Tahereh/Qorrat al-Ayn) has been published in volumes devoted to their work, and I have used these where they are available. For all other poets writing before the twentieth century I have in the main used the following anthologies (none of which are easy to find, and I am gratefully indebted to friends who procured me copies, as books, photocopies, or electronically):

Az Rabe'eh ta Parvin ("From Rabe'eh to Parvin"), ed. Kesharvarz Sadr (Tehran: n.d. [1950s]), 282 pp.

Az Rabe'eh ta Parvin ("From Rabe'eh to Parvin"), ed. Parvin Shakiba (Champaign, IL: 1998), 210 pp.

Four Eminent Poetesses of Iran: With a Brief Summary of Iranian and Indian Poetesses of New-Persian, ed. M. Ishaque (Calcutta: 1950), 100 pp.

Noql-e Majles ("Confection of the Assembly"), ed. Mohammad Reza Nasiri and Nadereh Jalali (Tehran: 2006), 69 pp.

Zanan-e Sokhanvar ("Eloquent Women"), ed. Ali Akbar Moshir Salimi, 2 vols. (Tehran: 1335/1956), 789 pp.

Zanan-e Sokhanvar o Namvar-e Afghanistan ("Eloquent and Famous Women of Afghanistan"), ed. Mohammad Halim Tanvir (Peshawar: 2001), 290 pp.

Although there is considerable overlap between these anthologies, so that frequently the same poets are cited and the same poems quoted (often in slightly different versions), each has its own usefulness. *Zanan-e Sokhanvar*, edited by Ali Akbar Moshir Salimi, is by far the most comprehensive of the group, with the largest number of poets and poems, and with a commentary on each poet where relevant information is available (virtually nothing, apart from their names, and sometimes not even that much, is known about a number of poets included in the book).

Kesharvarz Sadr's book, *Az Rabe'eh ta Parvin*, is similar to Salimi's. While it is considerably shorter and contains the works of fewer poets, its commentary on the poets it does contain is often more scholarly, extensive, and reliable than Salimi's.

Despite sharing the same title, Parvin Shakiba's *Az Rabe'eh ta Parvin* is a quite different work from Sadr's (although it reproduces one or two biographical passages from Sadr's book almost word for word). Shakiba discusses the poets included in a much more historically informed fashion than either Sadr or Salimi does, and is also concerned to point out the qualities that can distinguish poetry in Persian written by women from that written by men. Much of the book has, justifiably, a somewhat polemical tone; where relevant it emphasizes the moments when women poets complain about both their circumscribed social situations and their often reprehensible treatment by men.

Zanan-e Sokhanvar o Namvar-e Afghanistan, edited by Mohammad Halim Tanvir, is a rather peculiar book. Despite its title's claim to be specifically about Afghan women poets, it is, like the other collections mentioned here, an anthology of Persian-language women poets in general, and includes poets from Iran, India, and central Asia, as well as from Afghanistan. Its commentary is often politically quite tendentious, and it is by and large more of a patriotic publication than a scholarly one. However, it does include a number of genuine Afghan women poets, and examples of their poems, that are absent from the other anthologies listed here.

The poets who are the chief subjects of *Four Eminent Poetesses of Iran: With a Brief Summary of Iranian and Indian Poetesses of New-Persian* are Rabe'eh (tenth century), Mahsati (twelfth century), Tahereh/Qorrat al-Ayn (nineteenth century), and Parvin Etesami (twentieth century), all of whose work is available elsewhere. The "summary" mentioned in the subtitle is quite extensive and useful, and includes some poets not mentioned in other sources. The book is in English, with the poems in the book's main section given in Persian followed by generally reliable, if rather Victorian-sounding, English translations. Four poems by Mahsati, which the editor describes as "being grossly obscene," are given only in Persian. Two of the four deal with sex (one is the poem "The judge's wife was pregnant . . ." on p. 10) and the other two are scatological. By present-day standards none of these four poems would be considered "grossly obscene." The poems included as an appendix (the "brief summary" of the book's subtitle) are given only in Persian. The Indian compiler of the book, M. Ishaque, traveled to Iran in order to meet and if possible interview Parvin Etesami, but she declined to see him.

Noql-e Majles is a relatively short early nineteenth-century collection of brief lives of women poets, together with examples of their poetry, compiled by Mahmud Mirza, a son of the Qajar monarch Fath Ali Shah. Most of the poets included were members of the Qajar family (and so relatives of the compiler), although a number of earlier poets were also included.

The poem by Zinat Amin on p. 140 is to be found in:

Zanan-e Iran dar Jonbesh-e Mashruteh ("Iranian Women in the Constitutional Movement"), ed. Abdol Hossein Nahid (Tabriz: 1360/1981), p. 98.

Acknowledgments

It would have been impossible for me to produce this anthology without considerable help from a number of other people, for which I am extremely grateful. I am indebted especially to the writings of Ahmad Karimi-Hakkak on contemporary Persian poetry and to the writings of Sunil Sharma on Persian poetry in India, particularly but not exclusively during the period of the Moghul empire, and to both of them for conversations on poetry and related subjects over a number of years.

I am also personally indebted and grateful to the following colleagues and friends who have assisted me in a number of ways: Ehsan Yarshater, Asghar Seyed-Ghorab, Mandana Zandian, Azar Nafisi, Saeed Honarmand, Farzaneh Milani, Franklin Lewis, Ebrahim Paydar, Farshad Zahiri, Margaret Mills, Hasan Javadi, Ida Mirzai, Javad Ashrafi, and Mohammad and Najmieh Batmanglij. I must thank especially Fatemeh Shams, who has been indefatigably generous in the help she has given me over the section on contemporary poets and their poetry. My chief debt, as always in my translations of Persian poetry, is to my wife, Afkham Darbandi; I might have produced some kind of an anthology without the help of others I've thanked here, but without Afkham's continuous and unstinting assistance and support it is doubtful whether this anthology would exist at all.

A Note on Iranian Dynasties

Below are the dynasties mentioned in this book, arranged in approximate chronological order.

Sasanian. The Sasanians were the last pre-Islamic Iranian dynasty; they ruled Iran from 224 CE to 651 CE.

Seljuk. Originally Oghuz Turks from central Asia who invaded Iran in the first half of the eleventh century, the Seljuks ruled Iran in the second half of the eleventh and throughout most of the twelfth century.

Mongol. The Mongol conquest of Iran began with Genghis Khan, who conquered much of northern Iran in 1220 and 1221, a process continued by his grandson Hulagu between 1256 and 1258. Genghis Khan's conquest was undertaken for the purpose of plunder, but Hulagu settled in Iran and established an empire there. Hulagu remained culturally a Mongol until his death, and he died a Buddhist (his wife was a Christian). His descendants became Persianized, converted to Islam, intermarried with local ruling families, and were gradually absorbed into the general population.

Inju. A relatively short-lived minor dynasty of Mongol origin; the Injus ruled Shiraz and Esfahan during the fourteenth century.

Chupanid. Rivals of the Injus and, like them, a minor dynasty of Mongol origin, the Chupanids ruled parts of Iran in the fourteenth century.

Timurid. Descendants of Timur the Lame (Tamburlaine) who ruled much of Iran, Afghanistan, and southern central Asia from the mid-fourteenth to the late fifteenth century.

Safavid. Ruling Iran from 1501 to 1736, the Safavids declared Shi'ism to be the country's official religion. For most of their reign their capital was Esfahan, which they made into one of the most beautiful cities in the Middle East.

Ottoman. The dynasty that ruled Turkey and the Ottoman empire from 1299 to 1924.

Moghul. Founded in 1526 by the emperor Babur, who claimed descent from both Timur the Lame (Tamburlaine) and Genghis Khan. The Moghuls ruled northern India and much of the rest of the country until the last Moghul emperor, whose power was by this time largely titular, was deposed by the British in 1857.

Qajar. The dynasty that ruled Iran from 1789 to 1925. The last thirty years or so of the Qajar reign were marked by the struggles for representative government and political and economic independence from outside interference and control.

Pahlavi. The dynasty that ruled Iran from 1925 until the second Pahlavi king, Mohammad Reza Shah, was overthrown by the Islamic Revolution in 1979; since the Revolution, Iran has been governed as a theocratic republic.

Map Showing Places Mentioned in the Book

The Mirror of
My Heart

Map Showing Places Mentioned in the Book

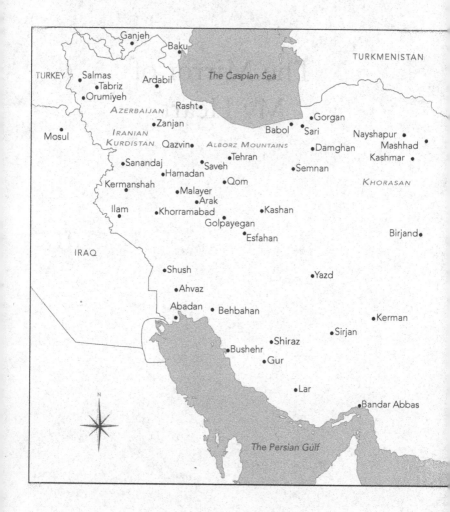

The Medieval Period

Rabe'eh
Tenth century

Rabe'eh's family claimed descent from Arabs who had entered Iran during or after the seventh-century conquest of the country. By the time Rabe'eh was born, her father had become ruler of Balkh in what is now northern Afghanistan. Almost no information about her life has come down to us, although the lurid story of her demise is well known: after her father died she is said to have carried on a secret love-affair with a slave or servant at what was now the court of her brother, Hareth. The liaison was discovered, and Hareth cut her throat and left her in a bath-house where she bled to death; her lover then killed Hareth and committed suicide.*

★

The garden shows so many flowers, as though
Mani had painted their resplendent glow

Dawn's breezes never bore Tibetan musk,
How is the world so musky when they blow?

---

*A similar story is told about the sixteenth-century Italian poet Isabella di Morra. From an aristocratic family, she is said to have been her father's favorite child; after his death she carried on a secret correspondence with a man with whom she was in love, and of whom her brothers disapproved. Her brothers intercepted the correspondence, had her lover killed, and then personally killed their sister.

Are Majnun's eyes within the clouds, that they
Shed Layli's cheeks' hue on each rose below?

Like wine within an agate glass, his tears
Have filled each tulip with their crimson glow

Raise up the wine bowl, raise it generously
Since bad luck dogs deniers who say "No"

Narcissi glow with silver and with gold
It's Kasra's crown their shining petals show

Like nuns in purple cowls the violets bloom
Do they turn into Christians as they grow?[1]

★

My hope's that God will make you fall in love
With someone cold and callous just like you
And that you'll realize my true value when
You're twisting in the torments I've been through.

★

His love has caught me once again—
I've struggled fiercely, but in vain.
(Well, sobersides, explain to me
Just who can swim love's shoreless sea!
To reach love's goal you must accept
All you instinctively reject—

See ugliness as beauty, eat
Foul poison up and call it sweet.)
I jerked my head to work it loose,
Not knowing all this would produce
Was further tightenings of the noose.

★

I'm drunk with love to know my love is here tonight
And that I'm freed from sorrow and from fear tonight;
I sit beside my love, and earnestly I say,
"God, make the key to morning disappear tonight!"

Mahsati

*c.*1089–1159

Mahsati was said to be from Ganjeh, in what is now independent Azerbaijan, and to have sought employment as a scribe at the court of the Seljuk king Sanjar, who ruled from 1118 to 1157. She became known as the writer of a considerable number of short poems, and it is likely that many otherwise anonymous poems from the medieval period that seemed to be by women became attributed to her.

★

As wounded, and caught in your snare—there's no one
   like me
As driven by you to despair—there's no one like me
So many, so eagerly, vie for your love . . .
As steadfastly faithful I swear—there's no one like me.

★

If you're a hypocrite, and bow your face in prayer—what
   use is that?
Once poison's reached into your soul, remedial care—what
   use is that?
Showing yourself to everyone as though you're virtuous
   and moral,
If you're all filth within, the spotless cloak you wear—what
   use is that?

Love makes a lion cower in its lair—
It is a sea of wonders, strange and rare;
At times its kindly ways delight our souls
At times the smell of blood is in the air.

★

O son of Ganjeh's preacher, my advice to you[2]
Is: "Take the wine glass in your hand, give joy its due . . ."
Your piety and heresy don't interest God—
Seek pleasure in this world now, while you're able to.

★

Come, I've prepared a private room where we can meet,
With precious cloths laid there, to make a snug retreat;
I've grilled kebabs and wine I want to share with you—
The wine is from my eyes, my anguished heart's the meat.[3]

★

I wish I were a shining thumb-ring,
            Such as our archers wear!
Each time he came to shoot an arrow
            He'd lean to me with care,
And as the bow-string reached his teeth,
            I'd steal such kisses there!

★

You think you'd like to sleep with me?
That's an impossibility!
No dream of yours could bring about
This idiotic fantasy;
What makes you think you might? Even
The winds of heaven can't get to me.

★

Great king, the heavens have saddled Glory for you—
More than all other monarchs, they adore you!
To keep your horse's golden horseshoes spotless
They've spread a silver carpet out before you.[4]

★

I said, "Quick, bring some wine." He said, "Look here,
It's Friday's eve; shouldn't you sleep, my dear?"*
I said, "Each week there'll be another Friday—
The roses bloom for us but once a year . . ."

---

*Friday is the Moslem holy day, and so a day on which wine should
certainly not be drunk. As in the Jewish calendar, the day begins at its
"eve," that is, sunset on the previous day.

★

Those nights when I so sweetly slept with you—they've gone.
Those pearl-like tears my lashes wept with you—they've gone.
You were my heart's peace and my soul's dear friend—you
    went,
And all the promises I kept with you—they've gone.

★

I knew your promises were feeble-hearted,
I knew you'd break them, long before we parted;
And all the nasty things you did at last—
My friend, I had foreseen them when we started.

★

We're drunkards, ne'er-do-wells, but kind and civil—
We're not the men for prayers and all that drivel.
Our judge thinks wine's a sin; we're petty thieves,
He filches orphans' wealth . . . so who's more evil?

★

The judge's wife was pregnant, he was furious,
"I'm old," he cried, "and this is more than curious!
That whore's no Virgin Mary, and my prick can't stir—[5]
So whose child is it then that's grown so big in her?"

★

I'm drunk, and drunkards are the crowd I follow—
Ascetics' claims I find absurd and hollow;
I love that moment when the server says,
"One more . . .?" and one more's more than I can swallow.

★

That handsome cobbler when he sews a shoe
Kisses the leather as he bites his thread—
A shoe that's kissed by such sweet ruby lips
Deserves to crown the sun-in-heaven's head.

★

It seems, my boy, you went out drinking wine last night
And thought that kissing someone else would be all right,
But in response, or so I hear, she scratched your face—
When do I get to see what must be quite a sight?

★

An old man says we must remain here—
       we can't be kept locked up
In this sad chamber, wracked with pain here,
       we can't be kept locked up
That woman whose tempestuous hair
       is like a wild beast's mane,
Stuck in the house, held by a chain here,
       she can't be kept locked up

Go, tell the bath-house owner that he needn't keep
His fire alight tonight, that he can go and sleep,
And in the morning I'll be there—my burning heart
Will be the fire, the water all the tears I'll weep.

*

I saw, dead drunk and stretched out in the lane, a man I
    know—
I lent a hand and helped him to his feet, and watched him go;
Today it seems he can't remember this, and looks as though
He means to say, "Do I know you?" It happened, even so.

*

His face is envied by both jessamine and rose,
His flirting charms both sexes everywhere he goes—
Lissome as flowing water, I saw him walking once . . .
And still within my eyes that gentle water flows.[6]

*

I wish I had the heart
        to write a letter and complain;
I wish I had the soul
        to find the right words for my pain—
I'm so distracted, crazed
        with wretchedness, I pick my pen
And paper up . . . and start to cry . . .
        and throw them down again.

★

Dear, dry your pointless tears, tears don't suit you—
I'm sad enough, you needn't be sad too;
Look, you're the loved one, crying's not your role—
Let *me* do what the lover has to do!

★

You're no great intellect, and men like you don't know
The usual kindnesses a lover ought to show—
My flighty friend, I'm glad I'm with you here tonight,
I hope I don't regret it in the morning though . . .

★

Although we don't get on in any way
I'll be polite to you still, come what may.
"What have I done?" you ask. Just tell me what
You haven't done! My dear, what *can* I say?

★

The one your beauty's overthrown
　　　　　　has come back home;
The one who thirsts for you alone
　　　　　　has come back home;
Prepare the cage again, scatter your seeds
　　　　　　of kindness there—
Look, broken-winged, the bird you own
　　　　　　has come back home.

★

A rose that's celebrated everywhere—that's something
A youngster's shirt disfigured by a tear—that's something
Sweating profusely, crimson-faced, confused with shame
A mouth that's stuffed with golden coins, I swear—that's
　something[7]

Anonymous
Twelfth century or earlier

Nothing is known about this poet, though her poem indicates that she was probably a female musician/entertainer.

★

Brought to this town's bazaar today, I'll be
The best "companion" here—so who will hire me?
Though I don't care for those who want to have me,
And those I like the look of don't desire me.[8]

Motrebeh

Twelfth century

Motrebeh is a description of her profession, as it means "a female musician," rather than her actual name, which is unknown. She was a member of the household of Toghan Shah, the ruler of Nayshapur, who died in 1185 or 1186.

*

I said, "My heart would like a kiss from you."
"A kiss from me will cost your soul," he said.
Immediately my heart poked at my side
And whispered, "That's dirt cheap, dear, go ahead!"

Daughter of Salar

Early thirteenth century

Referred to as *bint Esfahanieh* ("the woman from Esfahan"), the poet's given name is unknown. She became famous for a now lost panegyric she wrote to the Seljuk soltan Kay Kavus I, who ruled in Asia Minor in the first quarter of the thirteenth century, and this gives us the approximate period in which she lived. Her panegyric received this encomium: "The daughter of Hesamaddin Salar sent to his Majesty from Mosul this panegyric, which outdoes the gentle breeze of spring in its graciousness and the waters of Paradise in its flowing limpidity. His majesty gave instructions that she was to be paid a hundred dinars of red gold for every line. As there were 72 lines, 7,200 dinars were dispatched to Mosul . . ."*

★

The more I search myself the more I see
That longing for your love has ruined me;
I gaze into the mirror of my heart,
And though it's me who looks, it's you I see.

---

*The quotation is from the thirteenth-century anthology *Nozhat al-majales*, ed. Dr. Mohammad Amin Riahi (1366/1987), p. 69.

Aysheh Samarqandi

Thirteenth century

This poet's name is also given as Aysheh Moqrieh, "Moqrieh" meaning "a female singer." Apart for the fact that she was from Samarqand and lived as a singer, nothing further is known about her.

★

I said, "Bright moon, give my heart back to me—
How long must I endure love's agony?"
He spread a thousand hearts before my eyes
And said, "Take yours; which is it? You tell me."

★

My eyes weep pearl-like tears that glisten⁹
Like shining earrings in my ears—
So take these earrings, since the world
Says you're the owner of my tears.

★

Night's secrets in your arms have just begun
And night is over . . . here's the rising sun;
But still, I wouldn't take a hundred lives
In place of such a night, so quickly gone.

★

My hated love, last night, and all night too,
They—curse them—told me stories about you;
Their gossip was you break your promises;
And d'you know what? My heart said, "Yes, it's true."

Fatemeh Khorasani

Died 1246

The light-hearted frivolity of the few poems attributed to Fatemeh Khorasani is in stark contrast to the dramatic story of her life and death (recounted by the thirteenth-century historian of the Mongol empire, Jovayni). She had been captured as a slave during a Mongol raid on Khwarazm, and despite her lowly status became the trusted intimate of the Mongol queen Toregene, gradually replacing most of Toregene's ministers in the process and making a great many enemies at court. When Toregene died under suspicious circumstances, Fatemeh's enemies accused her of killing the queen by witchcraft. Tortured until she confessed to the crime, she was then drowned.

★

Kindness from you, and faithfulness, can't be expected,
Without your presence all life's pleasures are neglected . . .
Your being here's the water of eternal life
But, like that sacred stream, as yet it's undetected.

★

The blossoms return and the nightingales sing
Our wine-loving friends drink to welcome the spring
Without you our plans have all fallen apart
Just get yourself here, you're the one missing thing

Padshah Khatun
1256–95

A member of the Mongol nobility that ruled Iran in the thirteenth century, Padshah Khatun was famous for her verses, her beauty, and her ruthlessness. She was married twice, first to Abaka Khan (the great-grandson of Genghis Khan), who became the country's ruler in 1282 and died shortly afterward, and then to the crown prince, her stepson Gaykhatu, whom the fifteenth-century historian Mirkhond characterized as being too "addicted to wine, women, and sodomy" to rule, which meant that Padshah Khatun became the de facto head of state. As queen, she had her half-brother Suyurghatamish murdered, because he had forcibly taken over the rule of Kerman from Padshah Khatun's mother. Gaykhatu was assassinated in 1295, and factions supporting Suyurghatamish's widow had Padshah Khatun captured and killed.

★

I'm in my lover's alley, but he's gone—
On walls and doors his scent still lingers on

★

That apple you in secret sent to me
Gave with its scent eternal life to me—
My heart glows now like fire with happiness
That from your hand this gift was sent to me.

Possessed of untold sovereignty, beneath my veil[10]
I am a woman whose good deeds will never fail;
Even for breezes that the morning wafts to me
It's hard to pass the curtain of my chastity—
I keep my shadowed beauty from the sun, whose light
Illumines towns, bazaars, and every common sight.
Not every woman with two yards of veil can reign,
Not every crowned head's worthy of a king's domain—
I am descended from great kings, if earthly powers
Belong to anyone they are assuredly ours.

★

Although I am the child of powerful kings,
A fruit upon the Mongols' royal tree
Who's lived her life in luxury and laughter,
My exile now brings only tears to me.[11]

Delshad Khatun

Fourteenth century

Delshad Khatun was a member of the Chupan family, who were descendants of the Mongol conquerors of Iran, and major contestants in the power struggles that engulfed much of Iran in the fourteenth century. "Khatun" is a female honorific, indicating royal status.

★

The drops of sorrow Heaven rains on me
Have sent me wandering over land and sea—
Ah, would that they could bring me to the place
That frees me from this being that is me.

★

Now every difficulty in my heart
Has been resolved . . . a good result!
Except for one, since to resolve love's grief
Still proves to be too difficult.

Jahan Malek Khatun

c.1324–c.1382

An Inju princess, Jahan Khatun was the daughter of Masud Shah, the ruler of Shiraz and its environs from 1336 to 1339. Masud Shah was assassinated in 1342; his death was avenged by his brother (and Jahan Khatun's uncle) Abu Es'haq, who ruled Shiraz from 1343 to 1353. The fourteenth-century traveler Ibn Battuta describes Abu Es'haq as "one of the best of Soltans, handsome and well-conducted, of generous character, humble but powerful and the ruler of a great kingdom . . ." He was a major patron of poets and it seems likely that he encouraged his niece's poetic gifts. Jahan Khatun married her uncle's *nadim*, his bosom friend and drinking companion; if her poems are to be believed, the marriage was not a happy one. She had a daughter who died while still a young child, and about whom she wrote twenty-three elegies. In 1353 Abu Es'haq was overthrown by the warlord Mobarez al-Din, who killed the male members of Jahan's family; Jahan Khatun herself was imprisoned for a while and then driven into exile. With the accession to the throne of Mobarez al-Din's son in 1358, Jahan Khatun returned to Shiraz, where she lived out the rest of her life. Her extensive divan (collected short poems), containing over 1,500 poems, has survived in two complete and two partial copies, which means that we have more poems by her than by any other pre-twentieth-century woman poet who wrote in Persian.

★

I swore I'd never look at him again,
I'd be a Sufi, deaf to sin's temptations;
I saw my nature wouldn't stand for it—
From now on I renounce renunciations.

★

You wandered through my garden, naked and alone
(The roses blenched to see their beauty overthrown).
My cheeky love, your body is the Fount of Youth
(But in your silver breast your heart is like a stone).

★

Last night, my love, my life, you lay with me,
I grasped your pretty chin, I fondled it,
And then I bit, and bit, your sweet lips till
I woke . . . It was my fingertip I bit.

★

My love's an ache no ointments can allay now;
My soul's on fire—how long you've been away now!
I said, "I will be patient while he's gone."
(But that's impossible . . . it's one whole day now . . .)

I told my heart, "I can't endure this tyranny!
He's nothing, no one! What's this bully's love to me?"
My little heart, you're like a boundless sea, it seems;
And common sense? A splinter somewhere on that sea.

★

My heart, sit down, welcome love's pain,
           and make the best of it:
The rose is gone, the thorns remain,
           so make the best of it.
My heart said, "No! I can't endure
           this sadness any longer . . ."
I said, "You've no choice, don't complain,
           just make the best of it."

★

I feel so heartsick. Should my doctor hear,
He'll sigh and groan and want to interfere:
Come on now, dearest, heal me, you know how
To make my doctor's headache disappear.

★

Always, whatever else you do, my heart
Try to be kind, try to be true, my heart:
And if he's faithless, all may yet be well—
Who knows what he might do? Not you, my heart.

Shiraz when spring is here—what pleasure equals this?
With streams to sit by, wine to drink, and lips to kiss,
With mingled sounds of drums and lutes and harps and flutes;
Then, with a nice young lover near, Shiraz is bliss.

★

My heart, if you have words you need to say,
Be warned! Keep would-be confidants away.
Seek help from no one here: five times a day
The entrance to His court stands open. Pray.

★

I know you think that there are other friends for me than you:
                                        Not so.
And that apart from loving you I've other things to do:
                                        Not so.

Belovèd, out of pity, take my hand before I fall,
You think the world can give me other loves to cling on to?
                                        Not so.

You strike me like a harp, play on me like a flute—and now
You have the nerve to say that I have had enough of you?
                                        Not so.

What heavy sorrows weigh me down, and crush my abject
  soul—
Could anything be harder than your absence to live through?
                              Not so.

Your eyes are languorous and rob my wakeful eyes of sleep,
Are any curls as wild as yours, as lovely and untrue?
                              Not so.

You say my heart has not been hurt by your disdain. It has.
Has any lover suffered love's despair as I do now for you?
                              Not so.

You have so many slaves, all finer than I am, I know—
But can you point to one more wretched in your retinue?
                              Not so.

★

                When someone is imprisoned for a while[12]
          Men ask about his fate, and want to know his crimes;
                If someone accidentally says my name
          Fear makes him beg to be excused, a thousand times.

★

          A picnic at the desert's edge, with witty friends,
          And tambourines, and harps, and lutes, is very sweet.
          And if my lover, for a moment, should drop by
          I'd grill his liver with my body's fiery heat![13]

Come here a moment, sit with me, don't sleep tonight,
Consider well my heart's unhappy plight, tonight;

And let your face's presence lighten me, and give
The loveliness of moonlight to the night, tonight.

Be kind now to this stranger, and don't imitate
Life as it leaves me in its headlong flight, tonight.

Be sweet to me now as your eyes are sweet, don't twist
Away now like your curls, to left and right, tonight;

Don't sweep me from you like the dust before your door;
Dowse all the flames of longing you ignite, tonight.

Why do you treat me with such cruelty now, my friend,
So that my tears obliterate my sight, tonight?

If, for a moment, I could see you in my dreams
I'd know the sum of all this world's delight, tonight.

★

Here, in the corner of a ruined school
(More ruined even than my heart), I wait

While men declare that there's no goodness in me.
I sit alone, and brood upon my fate,

And hear their words, like salt rubbed in my wounds,
And tell myself I must accept my state:

I don't want wealth, and I don't envy them
The ostentatious splendor of the great.

What do they want from me though, since I've nothing?
Now that I'm destitute, and desolate?[14]

★

How long will heaven's heartless tyranny
Which keeps both rich and poor in agony

Go on? The dreadful happenings of these times
Have torn up by the roots Hope's noble tree,

And in the garden of the world you'd say
They've stripped the leaves as far as one can see.

That cypress which was once the cynosure[15]
Of souls, they've toppled ignominiously;

I cry to heaven above, again I cry—
How long will this injustice fall on me?

What can I tell my grieving heart that won't
Let dearest friends assuage its misery?

You'd say heaven's stuffed its ears with scraps of cotton
Simply to show that it's ignoring me!

★

Most people in the world want power and money,
And just these two; that's all they're looking for.

They're faithless, callous, and unkind—the times
Are filled with squabbles, insurrections, war,

And everyone puts caution first, since now
Few friends exist of whom one can be sure.

Men flee from one another like scared deer,
And for a bit of bread the rabble roar

As though they'd tear each other's guts apart.
And why are men determined to ignore

The turning of the heavens, which must mean
The world will change, as it has done before?

But in their souls they are Your slaves, and search
The meadows for the cypress they adore;[16]

My heart's an untamed doe, who haunts Your hills,
And whom no noose has ever snared before.

★

My friend, who was so kind and faithful once,
Has changed his mind now, and I don't know why;

I think it must be in my wretched stars—
He feels no pity for me when I cry.

Oh I complain of your cruel absence, but
Your coming here's like dawn's breeze in the sky;

That oath you swore to and then broke—thank God
It's you who swore, and is foresworn, not I!

I didn't snatch one jot of joy before
You snatched your clothes from me and said goodbye;

I didn't thank you, since I wasn't sure
You'd really been with me, or just passed by.

How envious our clothes were when we lay
Without them, clasped together, you and I!

Your curls have chained my heart up; this is right—
Madmen are chained up, as they rage and sigh.

They say the world's lord cherishes his slaves;[17]
So why's he harsh to me? I don't know why.

★

A happy heart's the place for plans and piety,
And wealth's a fine foundation for sobriety:
A weak and wasted arm can't wield a warrior's sword,
A broken heart can't act with cold propriety.

★

I didn't know my value then, when I
        Was young, so long ago;
And now that I have played my part out here,
        What is it that I know?

I know that, now that both of them have gone,
        Life's good and bad passed by
As quickly in my youth as dawn's first breeze
        Forsakes the morning sky.

How many ardent birds of longing then
        Were lured down from the air
By my two ringlets' curls and coils, to be
        Held trapped and helpless there!

And in youth's lovely orchard then I raised
        My head as prettily,
As gracefully, above the greensward there,
        As any cypress tree;

Until, with charming partners to oppose me,
        I took up lovers' chess,
And lost so many of love's pieces to
        My partners' handsomeness—

And then how often on the spacious field
        Of beauty I urged on
My hopeful heart's untiring steed, always
        Pursuing what was gone.

Now, as no shoots or leaves remain to me
        From youth, and youth's delight,
I fit myself in my old age to face
        The darkness of the night.

Laughing, the rose said to the nightingale one day,
"How long will you keep up this constant racket, pray?
I'm leaving here, I'll pack and I'll be on my way . . ."
Now don't you get ideas from what these roses say!

★

I am still drunk that you were here,
                              and you were mine,
And once again I stretch my hand out
                              for that wine;

As your drunk eyes could not bestir
                              themselves, I too
Can't move; as you love wine, I love
                              the wine that's you.

And I will ask the gentle morning
                              breeze to bear
A message to my love who has
                              such musky hair,

Since that black hair's sweet scent, from being
                              next to me,
Has made me like a musk deer come
                              from Tartary.[18]

I fainted when you were not here,

                    I could not stand—

Be with me now, my love, support me,

                    grasp my hand;

Oh I was so distracted, heartsick,

                    that I gave

My soul into your ringlets' snare,

                    I was your slave;

My eyes wept tears of blood while you

                    were never there,

My feet were shackled in your curls'

                    enclosing snare.

How sad my heart was then! But, God

                    be praised, relief

Has now arrived for me; I have

                    escaped from grief!

★

Your face usurps the fiery glow and hue

                    of roses;

And with your face here, what have I to do

                    with roses?

Your ringlets' fragrance is so sweet, my friend,

No fragrant rose-scent could entice me to

                    seek roses—

Besides, the faithless roses' scent will fade,
Which is a serious drawback, in my view,
                                        of roses;

And if the waters of eternal life
Had touched their roots, so that they bloomed anew,
                                        these roses,

When could they ever form a bud as sweet
As your small mouth, which is more trim and true
                                        than roses?

★

Tonight my heart's a bird that longs to dare
To fly to one place, and to hover there . . .
I told her, "Don't go flying to his street now,
Begging's the one thing that our king can't bear."

★

They say the man I love, my heart's delight,
Is ugly. They believe that? Well, they might . . .
No one but I could bear this weight of love—
That they don't find him handsome's only right.

★

For most of these long nights I stay awake
And go to bed as dawn begins to break;
I think that eyes that haven't seen their friend
Might get some sleep then . . . this is a mistake.

★

At dawn my heart said I should go
    Into the garden where
I'd pick fresh flowers, and hope to see
    His flower-like beauty there.

I took his hand in mine, and oh
    How happily we strayed
Among the tulip beds, and through
    Each pretty grassy glade;

How sweet the tightness of his curls
    Seemed then, and it was bliss
To grasp his fingers just as tight,
    And snatch a stealthy kiss.

For me to be alone beside
    That slender cypress tree
Cancels the thousand injuries
    He's meted out to me

He's a narcissus, tall and straight!
    And so how sweet to bow
My head like violets at his feet
    And kiss the earth there now.

But your drunk eyes don't deign to see me,
    Although I really think
It's easy to see someone who's
    The worse for love or drink.

And though it's good to weep beneath
    God's cloud of clement rain,
It's also good to laugh like flowers
    When sunlight shines again.

My heart was hurt by his "checkmate";
    I think I must prepare
To seek out wider pastures then,
    And wander off elsewhere.

Jahan, be careful not to say
    Too much; it's pitiful
To give a jewel to someone who
    Can't see it's valuable.

★

An elegy on the death of her infant daughter:

Your heart a rosebush, and your soul a cypress,
    Sweet pleasure's bud, fruit worthy of the spirit,
And I, a mother now without her child,
    Denied life's joy, and all life should inherit.

How men loved seeing what they'd never seen
    Till—like a fairy's child—she slipped from sight;
Don't criticize me when I weep, but think
    How Jacob wept for Joseph day and night.[19]

What wound is this, whose only balm is tears?
        What pain, whose cure's lamenting and distress?
I weep a flowing river, and Oman
        Has never seen these pearls that soak my dress.

While I have eyes within my head, and while
        My tongue is in my mouth, I'll always see
Her image in my eyes, and by my tongue
        Her name will be repeated constantly.

This grief's so scorched my heart that when I'm dust
        That dust will show my sorrow all too well;
My house that was a shining paradise
        Is darker now than any dungeon cell.

My heart was like a home that welcomed pleasure,
        Now only grief comes knocking at its door;
My suffering heart has borne so much it's like
        A storm-tossed boat that cannot reach the shore.

Prepare to quit this wretched hovel here,
        When autumn comes the nightingales are leaving;
It's Fate that heaps these sorrows on our heads,[20]
        You can't say Time's to blame when you are
                              grieving.

*

Another poem on the same theme:

My heart's new rose was snatched from me, and grief[21]
Replaced her, given by the hand of Fate—
But then my eyes saw Rezvan's kindness when,[22]
As she approached, he opened heaven's gate.

★

Another poem on the same theme:

My heart will take no drug to dull this pain,
The seal of sorrow's set, and will remain:
My heart could never tire of your sweet presence,
Absence is all my life can now contain.

★

Look at this garden of the world
To see what it devises next
And whose fate, out of all our fates,
        The world revises next

To see just who it is who'll drink
The draught of Being that brings night,
And who will suffer here hungover
        In morning's light

To see whose foot will step into
The snare that snapped shut means disaster,
On whose hand it bestows the jewels
        That make him master

To see whose lucky ears will hear
The noble psalms that David sang,[23]
Whose bitter soul will be consumed
      By sorrow's pang

To see how many of our friends
It will at last consign to dust,
Counting off lovely girls as well,
      Since it needs must

To see whose garden grows with hope
Until it glitters tulip-red,
Whose rosebush bears no buds, but only
      Sharp thorns instead

To see how many changeless Fate[24]
Throws down from thrones into the grave,
To see whose star of fortune now
      Begins to fade[25]

★

The roses have all gone; "Goodbye," we say; we must;
And I shall leave the busy world one day; I must.
My little room, my books, my love, my sips of wine,
All these are dear to me, they'll pass away; they must.

★

I'll leave this wretched hovel[26] when You tell me to
And then—perhaps—my heart's grief will be cleansed by
   You;
May all the tangled knots that have beset my life
Be tangled knots Your mercy prompts You to undo.[27]

Mehri
Fourteenth / fifteenth century

Also known as Mehr al-Nissa or Mehri-ye Heravi, she was an intimate of the Timurid empress Gowhar Shad, who was married to Shahrokh, the ruler of an empire that stretched from Herat to Samarqand. When Shahrokh died in 1447, Gowhar Shad became de facto ruler of the empire until her own death, when she was over eighty, in 1457.

Mehri was married to a court doctor who was much older than she was, and many of her poems complain about this. Some seem to imply that she had a lover or two, but this may be no more than convention. Mehri may well have known at least some of the poetry of Jahan Malek Khatun (p. 24) as Jahan's poems could have still been in circulation during Mehri's lifetime, and a court ruled by an empress like Gowhar Shad would be a likely place for a princess's poems to be valued.

*

Between us now, I feel there's no connection left,
No loyalty or kindness or affection left;
You've grown so abject and so old, you haven't got
The feeble strength to manage an erection left.[28]

*

In your distinguished house, the thing I thought to have—
                                        it isn't there;
The freedom my distracted spirit sought to have—
                                        it isn't there;
You say, "I've everything, I've untold wealth and luxury."
Oh yes, there's everything: but what I ought to have—
                                        it isn't there.

★

A young girl married to a man who's old
Will find—till *she's* old—happiness denied her;
Better an arrow pierce her side, they say,
Than have a husband who is old beside her.

★

We sleep together, and you never satisfy me;
I talk to you at night—your silences defy me;
I'm thirsty, and you claim that you're the Fount of Life—
For God's sake, where's the water then that you deny me?

★

An answer to an old man who proposed himself as her lover:

Good God, what do you think my flesh is? What?
It's handsome men I fancy, young and hot!
If I liked weak old men, why would I whine
About the one that I've already got?

*

I said, "I'm someone whom your eyes forget."
He said, "But you like others whom you've met."
I said, "I know you, you've no kindness in you."
His answer was, "No, you don't know me yet."

*

He asked if he might kiss my lips, although
Not which lips—those above, or those below?

*

Don't be deceived by sweet talk's pretty gifts—
Caressing words are what a wet-nurse gives
The baby when she has no milk to give.

*

No night is shorter than a night
                          that's spent with you
Since as you draw aside your veil
                          the sun shines through.

*

If I had known to draw my skirts back
                          from an old man's grasp,
Sorrow would not have grabbed youth's collar,
                          and undone its clasp.

*

With welling tears my eyes are always dim
And it's my heart that fills them to the brim;
What can I do . . . my friend is leaving me,
And all that's good or bad is following him.

*

Old men are cautious with themselves,
                          the young are more, "Who cares"?
It's older buildings that require
                          continual repairs.

*

Put up your tousled hair that hides
                              your features from my sight—
Give me my first glimpse of the dawn
                              in place of this dark night.

*

So, if my friend avoids my company,
                              he's telling me
That for the same price that he bought me he's
                              now selling me.[29]

*

I've found a drop of wine will soon resolve
Hard problems wise old men have sought to solve

I wished to tell a candle my heart's yearning
All that was in my heart was in its burning

At dawn I wept; the tulip red as blood
Told of a heart on fire, and roots in mud

The tales that nightingales and angels tell
Are but the magic of your glance's spell

I said I'd ask the learnèd and the wise
Why wine's so loved . . . and got absurd replies

A realm gazed wondering on your face, Mehri;
Alas, alas, for that realm's brevity!

Atuni

Fifteenth century

"Atuni" is the term for a woman who teaches girls reading, writing, and embroidery. The poet's actual name is not known. She was married to a cleric, Mulla Baqai, who was a friend of Mir Nezam al-din Ali Shir (1441–1501), a Timurid intellectual, poet, and mystic who lived in Herat, and this gives us approximate dates for when she was alive, and perhaps where she lived. Biographical notices that mention her say that she and her husband used to exchange insulting/joking poems with one another, and this is one such exchange.

*

Atuni to her husband:

Mulla, your teasing and your flirting's killing me—
Whenever will your tickling fingers let me be?
When night comes though, you turn your back on me,
    and sleep—
And all your back can give my heart is misery.

Her husband's response:

My friends, this crone has killed me with her tyranny
And her complaints about my sleeping back to me—
If I should doze a moment with my back to her
She pokes me with her finger till she wakens me.

And her response to his response:

My bedfellow has killed me with his lethargy,
His back's the only part of him I ever see;
He hasn't got the strength to lift a languid limb—[30]
Better two hundred blows than that back facing me.

Zaifi Samarqandi

Fifteenth century

Nothing is known about the poet's life, although the first poem given below suggests that she was married, very unsatisfactorily, and the second that she may have been more interested in a same-sex relationship than in being with her annoying husband. Her name suggests that she or her family were from Samarqand.

★

My love does nothing for you—it's too late;
Flabby old fool, you're in a wretched state.
And you've the nerve to threaten me with blows?
You haven't got the strength to stand up straight!

★

Beyond all other longings, Arezu, I longed for you—
I saw your face, how strong my longing grew, Arezu![31]

Ofaq Jalayer
Late fifteenth / early sixteenth century

Ofaq Jalayer's family were wealthy aristocrats attached to the court of the Timurid soltan Baiqara of Herat (r. 1469–1506). Her husband, Darvish Ali Ketabdar, was governor of Qom for a while and then of Balkh, and ended his life as a courtier of the first Moghul emperor, Babur (r. 1526–30). If she accompanied her husband during his frequent changes of employment, this may account for the second of the poems given here.

*

I've promised that I'll give up drinking wine,
        my noble cypress tree—[32]
Although you haven't promised yet you'll give up
        giving wine to me.

*

What's all this talk of exile
        as a tale of misery?
Your homeland's where you're happiest
        wherever that might be.

*

From 1500 to the 1800s

Pari Khan Khanom
1548–78

Pari Khan Khanom was the daughter of Shah Tahmasp (the second Safavid shah) and the sister of Esmail, one of the claimants to Tahmasp's throne. After her father's death she was briefly de facto ruler of Iran; during the succession struggles she backed Esmail, who briefly became the third Safavid shah; however, he was replaced after two years by his half-brother Mohammad Khodabandeh, whose mother, fearing Pari Khan Khanom's still considerable influence and power, had her strangled at the age of twenty-nine.

★

We cannot lean upon this world
        this emptiness that fades away
Bring wine my friend, we cannot change
        the destinies we must obey

We cannot build a house upon
        this flowing flood of emptiness
Or think of life eternal in
        this ruin where we briefly stay

It is your eyebrow's lovely curve[1]
        to which my heart bows down in worship
While this is so, my love, my words
        cannot be heartfelt when I pray

Oh but it's true, my dear, that when
        your time here's coming to an end
All Loqman's wisdom cannot save[2]
        your life upon that fatal day[3]

Dusti

Sixteenth century

All that we know about Dusti is that her father was named
Darvish Qayam Sabzevari.

★

To see that moon's disheveled hair's to be
In love with his hair's faithless heresy

O friends, what aching pain a lover feels—
When once it's caught her, there's no remedy

Don't look for sense or order from a lover,
She's given up on both of them; Dusti

Weeps tears like clouds in spring; and spring's clouds cease
Their weeping now, she weeps so copiously.

★

Though we were friends, at last our friendship ended—
    Alas, that it was you that I befriended.[4]

Golchehreh Beigum

1515–57

One of the daughters of the first Moghul emperor, Babur (r. 1526–30), Golchehreh Beigum lived most of her life in what is now Afghanistan. She died in 1557, during a visit to India with her sister Golbadan (p. 59).

★

He's lovely as a rose, and everywhere he goes
Girls crowd around to hear his jokes and witty scorn—
Well, as they say, there is no rose without a thorn.

Golbadan Beigum

*c.*1523–1603

The youngest daughter of the Moghul emperor Babur (r. 1526–1530) and the sister of Golchehreh (p. 58). One of the most admired and influential of the Moghul princesses, she wrote a biography, which is also partly an autobiography, of her brother Humayun. The elegant refinement of her court, her cultural interests, and her generous charitable endowments made her a model for many subsequent aristocratic Moghul women.

★

Be sure that girls who treat their lovers badly
Are apt to find their lives will end up sadly.

Bija Shahi
Sixteenth century

An Indian courtesan at the court of the Moghul emperor Akbar (r. 1556–1605). Bija Shahi was said to be very beautiful and was also known for her scabrous poems, one of which—making fun of Hakim Abul Fath, an Iranian doctor who had emigrated to India—is given here.

★

How long will you caress me mouth to mouth
Then shove your leather in me back to front?
If this is all your prick's inclined to do
I'd rather have your beard lodged in my cunt.

Bija Nehani Qa'emi

Sixteenth century

The poet's children were said to have settled in India, but nothing further is known about her.

★

I'm getting a divorce, and I'll be rid of you;
Damn you—I'll get two husbands, both of them brand new!
The first one will be young and handsome, the second
A burly Turkoman: the youth's for me, to do
What sprightly lovers do; the Turkoman's for you.[5]

Tuni

Sixteenth century?

Tuni's dates and provenance are unknown; there seems to have been a brief fashion for obscene poetry by women in the sixteenth century, and this perhaps approximately dates her.

★

To her husband, who preferred his male lover to her:

That nice young man of yours . . . how would it be
If one night I came with you, to make three?
You'd be on top, my dear, and have his ass
While underneath his prick would be for me.

Bibi Mah Ofaq

Possibly sixteenth century

This poet's dates and provenance are unknown.

★

After my husband has made love to me
                     I'm left unsatisfied,
Not for one night with him have my poor heart's
                     desires been gratified—
And then he says that I'm prohibited
                     from finding someone else . . .
May even heathens never be
                     so wretched and so mortified!

Hejabi

Late sixteenth/early seventeenth century

A contemporary of the Safavid king Shah Abbas (r. 1588–1629), Hejabi was from Golpayagan, near Esfahan, and was said to be very beautiful.

*

Your vow of chastity prevented my disgrace—
If you were mad enough that this were not the case
You would be guilty of an even worse disgrace[6]

Jamileh Esfahani
Late sixteenth / early seventeenth century

Like Hejabi (p. 64), the poet was a contemporary of the Safavid king Shah Abbas (r. 1588–1629). Esfahan was the Safavid capital, and her name suggests that she was perhaps associated with the court. She is also known by her pen-name, Fasiheh.

*

The day I sat down at love's feast I hesitated,
I was afraid that I'd be left alone at last—
Now I've grown old, and drunk the last drop of life's
   water,
How bitterly I look back, and regret my past.

*

Within the garden of my fate
       Only harsh thorns of sorrow grew;
And as they grew they pierced my heart
       Both bit by bit, and through and through.

*

I shan't sleep now in sorrow or in madness
Nor shall my heart sleep overwhelmed by sadness—
Your eyes have stolen sleep from me, your slave
Can never sleep now, even in her grave.

Nehani Shirazi

Sixteenth century

All that is known about Nehani Shirazi is that she was said to be an imitator of the poetry of the poet Jami (1414–92) and that she presumably came from Shiraz.

★

I saw her in a dream, and went mad for her sake—
How would it be if someone saw her when awake?

Nur Jahan
1577–1645

Nur Jahan was born in Qandahar, while her Iranian parents were on their way to India to seek their fortune; her father became a vizier at the court of the emperor Akbar (r. 1556–1605). In 1611 she became the twentieth and last wife of the Moghul emperor Jahangir (r. 1605–27), by which time she was already a widow of thirty-four. Beautiful, intelligent, and well educated, she was by far Jahangir's favorite wife, and exercised great influence at his court. After Jahangir's death in 1627, she was sidelined during the squabbles over the succession and spent the rest of her life in comfortable retirement from court politics. She died in Lahore, where she is buried in the Shahdara Gardens.

★

A pity that the Chinese mirror broke; but good,
A means of looking at myself is gone for good.

★

They say that with a gentle breeze
            the petals of a rosebud part—
A smile from my belovèd is
            the key that will unlock my heart.
The heart cares nothing for the rose,
            for color, scent, complexion, curls . . .
What captivates a lover's heart
            is kindness's bewitching art.

God help these silly bungling poets
In love with their incompetence!
They say their love is like a cypress
As noble in his elegance,
His face will certainly eclipse
The moon in her magnificence;
The moon's a disc compared to him
Imperfect in its radiance,
The cypress is no more than timber,
Uncut and of no consequence.[7]

                                         ★

My tomb's a stranger's, there are no lamps or roses here;
You'll find no moth wings, there are no nightingales to
    hear.[8]

                                         ★

I set fire to my soul when I assumed your name;
I'm like a candle self-consumed within its flame.

★

MARFA

1638–1704

Ramadan's gone, the new moon has resumed her reign—
The wine-shop's key was lost, but it's been found again.

Makhfi
1638–1701

The poet's real name was Zib al-Nissa ("Loveliest of Women"). She was the daughter of the Moghul emperor Aurangzib (r. 1658–1707) and sister of Zinat al-Nissa Beigum (p. 76). Her pen-name, Makhfi, means "hidden," and she occasionally puns on this. At one time she was engaged to the son of Dara Shukoh, but the marriage never took place, probably because of the opposition of Aurangzib, who was contemptuous of Dara Shukoh (his older brother, and the legitimate heir to the Moghul throne, whom Aurangzib had defeated in a civil war). For twenty years she was kept under house arrest, on the orders of her father, in the Salimgarh fort in Delhi. She never married, although stories circulated about various clandestine affairs, including with Aqel Khan, the governor of Lahore, with whom she exchanged some of the poems given here.

*

My heart, circle the heart, which is the hidden ka'bah—
That ka'bah was made by Abraham, this one by God.[9]

*

I flee from knowing others so much that
Even before a mirror my eyes stay shut.

★

Love came, and gave my harvest's wealth away for straw,
It gave my happiness away for half a sigh—
My crazy heart has bartered for a glance my soul,
My soul, which not a hundred worlds could hope to buy.

★

Love comes, and steals a wise man's common sense outright
(Thieves dowse the light first, to stay out of sight);
A blind man wouldn't hurt himself as I have done—
I'm in the house but can't locate its owner's light.

★

O waterfall, why do you groan incessantly?
Who's made your forehead frown like this in agony?
What dreadful pain is it that makes you constantly
Batter your head against a stone, and weep like me?

★

The governor of Lahore, Aqel Khan, was said to be so smitten with Makhfi that he sent her this poem:

I'll be your nightingale if I should see you in the garden
With others there I'll be your fluttering moth, if I should
 see you;
Showing yourself to be the shining light of an assembly—
Well, that's no good to me; it's in your shift I want to see you.

Makhfi sent back this answer:

> The nightingale forsakes the rose to see me in the garden,
> The pious Brahmin will forsake his idols when he
>   sees me—
> I'm hidden in my words, like scent within a rose's petal,
> Whoever wants to see me, it's in my words he'll see me.

★

Another exchange between Aqel Khan and Makhfi (again, Aqel Khan is pushing his luck by being a bit risqué, and again Makhfi is fending him off, this time with an implied insult):

> What feeds on nothing and will rise,
> And, standing, vomits, and then dies?

Makhfi sent back this answer:

> Women provoke this thing to stir . . .[10]
> Your mother's sure to know—ask her.

★

This time Makhfi initiates the exchange:

> Although my sensibility's like Layli's
>> My heart is like Majnun's and wants to roam—[11]
> I think of wandering in the wilderness . . .
>> But shame's the chain that keeps me here at home.

Aqel Khan tries to rise to the occasion:

> When love is young and new and innocent,
>> It's very true, shame might restrain it
> But when it's grown up, wild, and confident,
>> What shame or modesty could chain it?

But Makhfi isn't having it:

> Pure-minded folk are always circumspect,
>> And shame will keep them modest and discreet;
> But when a bird's as shameless as you are,
>> What shame could ever claim to chain its feet?

★

> May the arm break that hasn't clasped
>> its love in its embrace
> The eyes go blind that haven't loved
>> to see their loved one's face

A hundred springtime buds are here,
                    each opening with such
                                        beauty—
The garden buds within my heart
                    show no such glowing grace

My efforts are all over now,
                    and I can't even show
A fistful of the dirt from my
                    love's street—no, not a trace

For years blood gathers in the musk-deer's
                    navel till it's musk—
What's that to me? It's not the mole
                    upon my loved one's face.[12]

★

I'm upset with my heart, and with me she's the same,
We're stone and glass, and I'm to blame and she's to blame;
When, Makhfi, shall I reach the dwelling of my friend?[13]
The road ahead of me is dark . . . . my horse is lame.

★

I seem a fresh green leaf, but look inside—
The leaf there's red with blood and henna-dyed;
I am a princess sunk in poverty,
My name's the only lovely part of me.[14]

No shoot of joyful green grew from my being's soil,
My thirst was never quenched by happiness's wine—
The precious springtime of my life was spent in searching,
For all my efforts though, no wedding dress was mine.

Zinat al-Nissa Beigum
1643–1721

The second daughter of the Moghul emperor Aurangzib (r. 1658–1707) and sister of Makhfi [Zib al-Nissa] (p. 70), Zinat al-Nissa was known for her learning and piety, and refused to marry. In the last years of his life she was her father's closest companion, and became a discreet but effective power behind the throne. She was buried in a mosque that she herself had endowed, in Delhi.*

*

God's grace suffices me as my
      companion in the tomb; His cloud
Whose shadow rains down mercy is
      sufficient for me as a shroud.[15]

---

*Beigum is the female equivalent of the masculine honorific Beig, which in theory indicated aristocratic status though it was often used for any woman to whom the person making the reference intended to show respect. It is particularly common in Indian titles.

Soltan Daghestani

Eighteenth century

A contemporary of the last Safavid king, Soltan Hossein (r. 1688–1726). Soltan Daghestani lived through the conquest of Esfahan by Afghan forces in 1722, and the fall of the Safavid empire. She was the cousin of Valeh Daghestani, the author of one of the most important collections of biographical notices of poets, who died in 1766.

★

I knew how weak my lover's promise was,
I knew this handsome suitor was cold-hearted,
And finally he left me in love's autumn . . .
I knew spring's fickle habits when we started.

Agha Beigum

Eighteenth century

All that is known of Agha Beigum is that her family was from Khorasan, in northeastern Iran, and that her father's name was Mohammad Khan Torkman.

*

In this world all the sane and sensible I see are sad;
But madness is another world than theirs—my heart, go mad!

Hayati

Eighteenth century

A contemporary of Karim Khan Zand, the ruler of much of Iran from 1751 until his death in 1779.

★

There is no sympathizer here to sympathize
There is no confidante in whom I can confide
There is no friend who'll offer friendship to me here
Though friends abound, and all around, on every side

★

Pecking for seeds within this dusty cage,
You say your nest in heaven is what you mourn for—
Break the cage open then, and spread your wings,
Fly to the heavenly gardens you were born for.

★

I'm wretched, and to cheer me up
              he knows what he should do;
Deliberately he acts as though
              he hasn't got a clue.

Aysheh Afghani

Eighteenth century

Aysheh Afghani was a contemporary of the Afghan king Timur
Shah Durrani (r. 1772–93); her son Faiz Talab took part in Timur
Shah's attempt to conquer Kashmir, and was killed in battle. She
is the first important woman poet writing in Persian who would
have thought of herself as an Afghan (until the eighteenth century,
western Afghanistan was seen as part of Iran, while the eastern
area of the country was seen as Indian).

*

I saw the sunset in the sky
　　at evening prayer time, tulip red—
It was as though they'd killed the sun
　　and there her blood-soaked skirts were spread.[16]

*

My Love was here; but there was no one here, that day;
Gently His strong grip snatched my wounded heart away—

And when the One who stole my heart unveiled His face
The angels and mankind knelt down before such Grace.

I slept, and in my dream a flower-filled garden shone;
I started up from sleep—all trace of it was gone.

That day, I handed Him my vow of slavery;
The pens of angel scribes recorded it for me.[17]

★

The things your sweet voice says   have killed me
The black eyes of your gaze . . .   have killed me

And by your wine-red lips I swear
Your teasing, coy delays . . .   have killed me

Your stature like a cypress tree's,
Your curls' enchanting maze . . .   have killed me

Your face—a candle in the night—
Your kindness and your praise . . .   have killed me

Your sweet-talk and your sugared lips
Your ceremonious ways . . .   have killed me

Your face's flower-like scents that leave
Me wondering in a daze . . .   have killed me

Don't be so proud of your cruel beauty
Your arrogant displays . . .   have killed me

You look on Aysheh with contempt—
How much your hard heart weighs . . .   it's killed me

★

A lament for her son:[18]

Are you content that I've a gaping wound
Piercing my gut, that I'm without my son?

My lacerated breasts, my eyes all tears,
They're all for Faiz Talab, my absent one.

The heavens' cruelty means I only see
Donkeys and cows—how long must this go on,

Now that I'm separated from my lion,
My only lord, my mighty champion?

I'm like Farhad, striking an ax against[19]
My forehead, in despair for what has gone;

At dawn, in my love's gardens, I shall be
A nightingale with my lamenting song.

I'm drowned within a sea of grief and sorrow,
Trapped in this misery that's never done;

Aysheh! How long shall I lament and moan,
Going from door to door, without my son?

Reshheh

Late eighteenth/early nineteenth century

Well known for her poetry in her own lifetime, she was the daughter of the period's most famous male poet, Hatef Esfahani (d. c.1783).

★

I've put up with a lifetime of your tyranny,
              hoping for your fidelity,
And now my life's gone by, and faithfulness from you
              was never once vouchsafed to me.

From all the world I chose you; now, too late, I see
              what recompense was given me—
It's that I hear the scorn and blame of all the world
              deriding and reviling me.

And if it's true that handsome lovers' promises
              are weak and broken easily
I've never seen or heard, my love, of any vow
              as weak as that you made to me.

My stony-hearted love, you broke my heart, but I've
              kept faith with you unceasingly
And I have never taken back my love for you,
              although you have abandoned me.

You pierced me with the arrow of your callousness
                    while I lay weeping piteously—
What was my sin but this, that I put up with all
                    your cold hard-heartedness to me?

And since I drank the wine of your first kindness down
                    it's never happened that I see
My glass of pleasure empty of that poisoned drink
                    my loving you has poured for me.

So what has Reshheh gained from all the benefits
                    his cloud of gifts has rained on me,
Now that the lightning of my grief has burned
                    the fields I planted once so hopefully?

★

How would it be if you should take from me
The anguish that I suffer secretly
By whispering as secretly to me,
By talking to me with sweet sympathy?

Your kindness wouldn't hurt the flowers you see,
Nor would the nightingale give up its song
If you should sit here on the grass with me
And show me truly you're aware of me

My helpless heart's endured your tyranny
And it could be that it is leaving me—
My soul is ready to depart I know
From all the cruelty you inflict on me

If, out of kindness, like a cloud you'd give
A little water to my hope's palm tree
I wouldn't want the showers of spring, or fear
The harm that autumn's winds might bring to me

If I were like Reshheh, in agony
Because you were so far away from me,
You'd never know the grief the world can give
If from this anguish you'd deliver me

★

My heart beats wildly in my breast as though
Pierced by a shaft shot from his eyebrows' bow.

Maluli

Late eighteenth / early nineteenth century

Maluli lived in Shiraz, and was a contemporary of the Qajar monarch Fath Ali Shah (r. 1797–1834).

★

If I don't like my friends, and choose
To make friends with my enemies—what's it to you?

If I spend time with who knows who,
It's me who's hurt if someone sees—what's it to you?

If I should hide my face away
From pestering acquaintances—what's it to you?

If one day I confide to strangers
My privacies and secrecies—what's it to you?

"Where are you going now?" To one
Who has my heart's allegiances—what's it to you?

"And now where are they taking you?"
To gardens and to shady trees—what's it to you?

How often you say, "Don't drink wine
With strangers!" I'll drink just as I please—what's it to you?

And if I tell both friends and strangers
My innermost anxieties—what's it to you?

If day and night Malul endures[20]
A lover's endless agonies—what's it to you?

★

My wretched heart's been captured by a heathen—[21]
What can I do, O God, in my despair?
I say God bless the dervishes, for whom[22]
This faith or that is neither here nor there

★

My little house shines brightly now my lover's here . . .
I wish
And friends surround me with their laughter and good
  cheer . . .
I wish

Would that I'd patience now my lover's far away
Or that his heart felt pity for his lover here . . .
I wish

Would that I wore a Christian's belt, and I were drunk,[23]
Hungover in a wine-shop, with my lover near . . .
I wish

If you would be my nurse and doctor, O my love,
I'd stay unwell forever just to keep you here . . .

> I wish

And then perhaps you would perceive my pain and ask,
"But when was your poor heart so badly hurt, my dear? . . ."

> I wish

I dreamed of you last night, that other girl was with you—
My luck that's half asleep might wake and reappear . . .

> I wish

Would that I weren't lamenting like a nightingale
Or that you were among the flowers I sing to here . . .

> I wish

You act so cruelly to your Maluli, and why?
Strangers should treat each other well, and be sincere . . .

> I wish

★

How long will you torment me in this way,
Making my heart more wretched every day?
If, in this night of sorrow, I should die—
Tell me, on Judgment Day, what will you say?

Effat

Born in 1798

Effat was a native of Shiraz but very little is known about her otherwise. The author of a book of short literary biographies, Mirza Ali Akbar Navab Shirazi, wrote of her, "Although she had had no teacher, and had not been instructed in the rules of poetry and poetics by any authority, due to her instinctive ability she was able to produce verses that are both eloquent and correct.",*

★

Did roses take his body as their pattern for such loveliness,
Or did his body imitate the graceful beauty they possess?
Did his disheveled hair learn all its tumbling curls from
   hyacinths,
Or did the hyacinths see him and imitate each tangled tress?
Did I learn from the gardens' birds my anguished songs and
   heartfelt cries,
Or did the birds learn all their songs from me bemoaning
   my distress?

---

* Quoted from "Tazkireh-ye Delgoshah," in *Zanan-e Sokhanvar*, ed. Ali Akbar Moshir Salimi, vol. 1 (Tehran: 1335/1956), p. 332.

Agha Baji
Died 1832 or 1833

One of the many wives of Fath Ali Shah (r. 1797–1834), though little else is known about her.

*

How fortunate that man is who contrives to dwell
Where you dwell, where the weather's fine, and all is
　well . . .
He's gone; my heart's the bell hung from his camel's neck,
Since custom says a camel has to have a bell.

Qamar Qajar

Nineteenth century

The poet was a member of the Qajar ruling family. Nothing
further is known about her.

*

O hunter, I'm a bird with torn wings, caught within your trap—
If you throw stones at me, my wings can't fly, or even flap.

*

I don't say, "Don't be so unjust to me"—
My heart rejoices that you think of me.

Esmat Khanom

Nineteenth century

One of the daughters of Fath Ali Shah (r. 1797–1834). The poem given here is an elegy for a young Qajar prince, though it is not known which one (there were a great many of them).

★

What have you done, cruel heaven, that you can never rest
From seeking to destroy the bravest and the best?

Is tyranny the only ware your stall has sold?
Are spiteful deeds the only food your scrip can hold?

Have you no wish to see a moon traverse the skies?
Have you no wish to see a shining sun arise?

How many wounded hearts you torture and oppress,
How many helpless hearts are filled with your distress!

May your soul mourn, like mine, throughout eternity,
Your spirit always groan, like mine, in misery.

Jahan Khanom

Nineteenth century

The poet was a granddaughter of Fath Ali Shah (r. 1797–1834) and the mother of Naser al-Din Shah (r. 1848–96).

★

A man or woman who is wise will be
Honored in every place and company—
A man or woman who knows nothing shows
That he or she's a thorn without a rose.

Efaf

Nineteenth century

Efaf was a cousin of Fath Ali Shah (r. 1797–1834), to one of whose sons, Haydar Qoli Mirza, she was married.

*

In love's street, O my heart, beware—
Highwaymen wait in ambush there.

*

Though I'm a bird trapped in a hunter's snare, I see
No difference in myself from any bird that's free.

Fakhri

Nineteenth century

Fakhri was one of the many daughters of Fath Ali Shah
(r. 1797–1834).

*

O nightingale, why sing so sadly to the rose
Which neither cares nor knows about your heartfelt woes?

*

They say love's a catastrophe . . .
O God, may no one ever be
Deprived of this catastrophe.

*

He said, "Forget the notion that I'll ever be with you."
I answered, "Giving up one's soul's the hardest thing to do."

*

The young folk make a fuss and flaunt themselves, while I
Watch jealously; I'm old, and feel it's time to die.

Mariam Khanom
Nineteenth century

The poet was the daughter of Mirza Abul Qasem Farahani (1779–1835), the reformist vizier of Abbas Mirza. When Abbas Mirza's son Mohammad Shah Qajar (r. 1834–48) was crowned as shah, he at first promoted Farahani to the post of chancellor of Iran, but shortly afterward had him executed. The poem given here may be a covert commentary on her father's betrayal and death.

★

Treat all men well, as far as you are able to,
May those who have deceitful hearts not injure you;
Don't trust the ones who seem so kind and beautiful—
O God, those men one shouldn't trust, the things they do!

Mastureh Kurdi
1805–48

Although she was ethnically a Kurd, Mastureh wrote her poems in standard Persian (rather than in Kurdish). She was a prolific poet, able to write fluently in a number of poetic genres. Her husband, Khosrow Khan, of whom she seems to have been very fond, was the governor of Sanandaj, the capital of Iranian Kurdistan.

★

Look at that fairy being, how gracefully he goes,
To seek out hearts to plunder, untiringly he goes—
Oh, woe to those who find themselves in love with him,
A Turk who's bloodthirsty, avid for loot, he goes;
No pity's yours at last, my stony-hearted love,
Given the way in which my wretched fortune goes.
The cypresses and pines bow down their towering crests
In every meadow where that lofty cypress goes;
Grief-stricken by her need for you, poor Mastureh,
Distracted in love's desert, weeping, wild, she goes.

★

Forget that Ramadan is here—today
Autumn has come: "Bring wine," the meadows say.

Our ancient sage's fatwa's in agreement:
"Drink goblets filled with flowing wine, and pay

No heed to sermons' cant." Come, pour the wine
That fills my soul with wonder and dismay—

The man who doesn't drink in autumn's not
A man but some ferocious beast of prey

I'd give the world's wealth for a drop of wine—
I'd give both worlds, and throw in Judgment Day.

Don't think it's only wine that's made me foolish—
Your eyes leave all my thoughts in disarray

The morning breeze is filled with musk's sweet scent
It seems you must have combed your curls today

Dear Rose, I think of how your petals fall,
And tremble like a tree the winds of autumn sway;

Be kind, and glance at me for once; I've spent
My life in wondering how you fare each day.

★

For one as sad as I am,
                    wine's a licit thing
And more so since fresh flowers
                    are blooming and it's spring

Your lips are ruby-red,
                    you are so pure a creature,
What words could paint such color,
                    or dare define your nature?

My friends, look well at this
                    cruel rogue—and understand
It's my shed blood that makes
                    the patterns on his hand[24]

You left, and with you went
                    my strength and good sense too,
Come back—my eyes weep tears,
                    my heart weeps blood for you

But don't complain about
                    his cruelty, Mastureh—
Our stony-hearted lovers
                    always act this way.

★

Flute-like, while you're away, I will complain tonight[25]
And I'll get drunk on wine to ease my pain tonight

And, oh, for God's sake don't advise me to stop crying
My sobs will be the flute's and tambourine's refrain tonight

Cruel friend, if not for your hot brand upon my heart
I wouldn't weep and call for you in vain tonight

But if my Khosrow should come home to visit me[26]
Like Jamshid I'll rejoice—laughter will reign tonight!

That king and I, we're one another's qebleh now,[27]
And it's to him that I will pray again tonight

★

The candle-brightness of your face has filled
   The cottage of my heart with light tonight

The gaudy splendor of its festival
   Has moved the angels with delight tonight

Hyacinths scent your shoulders, and you'd think
   This world's where musk and rose unite tonight

Thanks be to God, your face's sun has made
   My ruined heart the safest site tonight

My hands are filled with love to welcome him
   Within my soul the moon shines bright tonight

Don't criticize the words I use—he's here
　　Joy makes me stammer as I write tonight

Now Mastureh is in her lover's arms
　　No roses rival such a sight tonight

★

If my harsh Layli's heart were not so pitiless
I wouldn't be Majnun stuck in this wilderness[28]
If I could get the business of my heart in order
The pages of my mind would not be in this mess
If you would show your lovely face to pious preachers
We'd hear no more about true faith and faithlessness
If you would be the doctor for my heart's complaint
I'd need no medicines, and I'd quickly convalesce!
If Mastureh's love-longing could be made to end
She wouldn't sing these songs of her unhappiness

★

We've gone, we left behind us nothing good
And what we have to show on Judgment Day
Was built on water as it flows away

Why do we boast about this world of dust?
Tomorrow we ourselves are dust and clay

We did so many things we shouldn't do,
And planted thorns of sin along the way

We don't deserve caresses, we've no beauty,
It's not in heaven the likes of us will stay

Say that we're pious, but don't mention mosques
It's not to Mecca that we bow and pray

The elders in the church and synagogue—
These are the guides we follow and obey[29]

Why should the Friend inquire of us the good
And ill we've done, on Judgment Day?

The good in us is all from Him, likewise
The evil in us is from Him, we'll say.

O God, my heart and I took all the world
To write about, and let our spirit stray
From Him, the Friend, from whom we looked away.

★

Making Do

I'll pick weeds if no flowers appear for me
And I'll drink drops if I can't reach the sea.

★

Dear love, dear silver-chin, when you're not there[30]
My thoughts become as tangled as my hair—
If longing for you leaves me for a moment
My soul will leave my body then, I swear.

★

Your mouth is sweet and I'm embarrassed by my bitter
  words—
My letter was uncalled for, I accept that I'm to blame,
I feel degraded, mortified, and stuck in my own mud,
Unless your kind benevolence absolves me of my shame.

Mastureh Guri
1832–67

The poet lived her whole life in Gur, in northern Afghanistan,
and died unmarried at the age of thirty-four.

★

The lover's heart is drunk, around your face it's dancing
A candle around which two hundred moths are dancing

Wherever light that emanates from God is found
One in a mosque, another in a wine-shop, is dancing

And in an idol's temple was your beauty painted?
I see the idol and the temple, both are dancing

The preacher told me yesterday to give up love
Today he broke his oath, and drunkenly he's dancing

My heart sees both your curls' snare, and your pretty mole—
It trembles at the snare, around the mole it's dancing

And has the morning breeze passed through your lovely
    tresses?
In gardens nightingales, in ruins owls, are dancing

Behind the veil the banner of my love is streaming
Look, at its sound, crazed Mastureh is wildly dancing[31]

Shah Jahan Beigum of Bhopal
1838–1901

On the death of her father, when she was six years old, Shah Jahan Beigum became the titular ruler of the Indian state of Bhopal, although her mother acted as regent until her death in 1868, when Shah Jahan took over the government. She had been trained to rule, and did so wisely and well. Among the many public projects with which she became involved, she was one of the founders of Aligarh University, the most important Moslem university in India. Her first language was Urdu, in which she wrote her autobiography, but she also wrote poetry in Persian (as was not uncommon for educated Urdu speakers; one of the most admired Urdu poets, Iqbal (1877–1938), wrote a number of poems in Persian).

*

O Shah Jahan, your long life's many sins are great,
They're like a sepulcher that's dark and desolate;
But don't lose hope, your Judge is merciful—to Him
A single straw outweighs your sinful mountain's weight.

*

If some sweet, cypress-bodied youth should saunter past my grave,
I'm happy from my grave to wish him well, and others living too;
O heavens, how did you deal with Solomon and Alexander
That Shah Jahan should ever hope for happiness from you?

Baligheh-ye Shirazi

Nineteenth century?

This poet was presumably from Shiraz, but her dates are unknown.

*

At night a dog sleeps in your alleyway[32]
By day the sunlight kisses where he lay

From the 1800s to the Present

Tahereh
1814–52

Educated by her father, Tahereh—also known as Qorrat al-Ayn—
became a proselytizer for the teachings of a religious reformer,
Mirza Mohammad Ali of Shiraz, known as the Bab ("the Gate"),
the founder of Babism, a development of which became the
Bahai religion. The followers of the Bab were regarded by
orthodox Moslems with hostility that often turned violent,
and this was exacerbated by an attempt on the life of the then
shah, Naser al-Din Shah, in 1852, which was blamed on a Babi
conspiracy. Tahereh was among those killed in the reprisals against
the Babis; she was strangled, perhaps on direct orders from the
shah himself.[1]

★

If I should ever see you, face to face, and eye to eye,
I'd tell you of my sorrow, point by point, and sigh by sigh;

But like the wind I seek you, searching where we might meet,
Searching from door to door, from house to house, from
   street to street.

Searching for that small mouth, the scent that cheek bestows,
Searching from bud to bud, from flower to flower, from
   rose to rose.

My heart's blood spills as tears that fall unceasingly,
Flowing from creek to creek, from stream to stream, from
   sea to sea.

My life is woven through with love; the broken heart you left
Is yours now—thread by thread, and warp by warp, and
  weft by weft.

Tahereh found within her heart, searching it through
  and through,
From page to page, from fold to fold there, you, and only you.[2]

★

Oh, by your hair, I swear, you're my despair[3]
I moan aloud you're absent and elsewhere
Your ruby lips are my sweet honeycomb
And head to foot I'm gripped within love's snare

  I've gone and you are here in place of me

Although I've borne such grief for you, although
I've drunk repeated glasses of love's woe,
Although my soul is burned, worn out with pain
And dead with grief, my heart's alive, I know

  Because your lips like Christ's awaken me[4]

I am a treasure, one that's yours alone.
I'm silver, and the mine's a mine you own
I am a seed, you are the harvest's lord—
If you are me, what is my flesh and bone?

  If you are me, what's this misshapen me?

Your love's reduced me to a speck, and I
Am drunk with love for you; suppose that my
Poor hand should touch your hair with reverence—
Since you are me it's me I'd glorify

       My prayer mat has become my limbs for me

If my heart's yours, why hurt it as you do?
And if it's not, why's it so wild for you?
Moment by moment make this heartache greater
And drive this me from me now through and through

       Reside in this distracted heart that's me

The smoky fire of love's intensity
Has burned all that there's ever been for me,
It's cleansed belief from me and unbelief—
Your eyebrow's curve has all my piety

       And church and ka'bah are now one to me[5]

That day the world was made, creation's pen
Wrote on its tablets all the fates of men—
Before they came out from their nothingness
And life was breathed into their bodies . . . then

       Your seal was on the wild heart that's in me

Fate saw to it, when man was made from clay,
Your love was planted in my heart that day—
My love for you became my destiny
And heaven and hell for me have fled away.

       Apart from you there's no desire in me

We're what's left of ourselves, we die, the wine
We drink down to its last dregs is divine;
We're burned within bewilderment's deep valley,
We're lost souls wandering without a sign

How deeply will my shame dishonor me?

From when I cried out, "Show my truth to me!"
I've boldly walked his street for all to see—
I wandered everywhere and cried aloud
That he is all of me and I am he.

I am the heart, and he has taken me

My ka'bah is the dust upon your street,
Your face the light that makes the world complete—
My soul lives from the curling of your locks
My heart prays now to where your eyebrows meet.

Your curls are like the Christians' cross for me[6]

I'm wild with longing for my champion,
For my incomparable, my dearest one
A traveler in the valley of despair,
I long for only you, all else is gone.

Love fills my limbs now and is all of me

How long must I assent to what I hate
And hide the turmoil of my inward state?
And never mention that you're far from me,
And hypocritically preach and prate?

How long must longing be the sum of me?

My cloak and prayer mat? They're no longer mine—
I'll fill bright crystal glasses with red wine,
All Sinai's valley will be filled with light
And ardent love will make the whole house shine

      The wine-shop's door will be the place for me

My love of knowledge hurts and humbles me
I cry for justice now incessantly
My love has filled my glass with truth's pure wine . . .
From self and from the world I am set free

      The search for truth is what possesses me

The servant poured wine on the world's first day
And filled each glass that leads our minds astray
And essences were accidents, reduced
To drunken nothingness and swept away

      The wine itself is drunk that is in me

At every moment love resumes its call
It summons all the world and all in all—
Whoever wants to walk this way with me,
If waves of ruin make him fear to fall

      He shouldn't venture near this sea that's me

Up on the roof now, there and everywhere,
I am your maid, a bird trapped in your snare,
And I'm the owl that calls to you at night—
My life depends upon your being there

      The pain of being me has gone from me

Shahdokht

Nineteenth century

Shahdokht lived in Malayer, in western Iran. The colloquial language in Malayer is Luri, and the fact that she wrote in Persian suggests that she was well educated, and perhaps not from a local family. The twentieth-century scholar Ali Akbar Moshir Salimi has suggested that her family may have been a provincial branch of the ruling Qajar dynasty.*

★

Each night, because of you, my teardrops fall
And lie like pearls upon my dress and shawl
And since there's no man in these parts who's faithful,
Shahdokht's decided she won't wed at all.

★

I am a girl well versed in poetry,
I am my generation's Mahsati—[7]
My boast is that I've left the world behind;
A virgin still, at thirty—this is me.

---

*Ali Akbar Moshir Salimi, ed., *Zanan-e Sokhanvar*, vol. 1 (Tehran: 1335/1956), p. 286.

Soltan

Mid/late nineteenth century

The daughter of Mahmud Mirza, the eldest son of Fath Ali
Shah (r. 1797–1834), Soltan grew up in a literary family, and
one perhaps especially favorable to the writing of poetry by
women, since her father was a well-known poet and calligrapher
who wrote various books on literary subjects, including one on
women poets.

*

Whilst I can think of you, and wander in your street,
     I don't want paradise
What houri could compare with you? Beside your street
     what heaven could suffice?

*

Watch how it is that I pass by his street, my heart—
With laughter I arrive, with weeping I depart.

*

That man whom no one's ever seen
     caught by a lover
I'll catch him yet; his vaunted freedom
     will be over.

Gowhar

Mid/late nineteenth century

Gowhar was a granddaughter, through her mother, of Fath Ali
Shah (r. 1797–1834). A book of her poetry was published in 1901;
as the book was not compiled by her, this suggests that she had
died by this time.

★

What I most value from my life was mine last night,[8]
My lips touched his sweet lips until the dawn's first
   light;
My candle guttered, but until the morning broke
The sunlight, moonlight, starlight made my pillow
   bright.
My lap was filled with tulips from a sheaf of flowers,
His tumbling curls made me a necklace of delight;
No one can know the heavenly things I saw from him—
The sum of life, of all the world, was mine last night.
I kissed his hair and smelled his hair so constantly
My breath was musky from his hair's sweet scent last
   night.
I fainted from his scent, and this is no surprise—
I clasped a sheaf of flowers till dawn assailed my sight.
At times my bolster was narcissi piled together,
At times my pillow was his curly locks last night;
Gowhar, he gave your heart's desire, and took your soul—
My love can't say the bargain wasn't fair, last night.

★

Although we never act as You have told us to
We're always seated at the feast prepared by You—
We eat there all the time, since from the first we knew
Your mercy's something You continually renew.

Gowhar Beigum Azerbaijani
Nineteenth century

The poet's dates and provenance are unknown, though her name suggests that she or her family came from Azerbaijan in northwest Iran.

★

If I should let the wind caress my hair,[9]
Its scent would lure wild deer into my snare

If I should pass a church one day, the vision
Would draw the Christian girls to my religion.

One glance of mine will make two hundred men
Whom death has taken, come to life again

Let Jesus know my miracles, inform
Him of the wondrous deeds I can perform.

Shahin Farahani
1864–1919

Shahin Farahani was a member of the same politically active family as Mariam Khanom (p. 96); her brother, Adib al-Mamalek Farahani (1860–1917), was a well-known poet and journalist who often expressed support for patriotic and liberal causes in his writings during the period leading up to the Constitutional Revolution of 1905–11.

*

My greetings to you now, women who are concerned
for our country
Women bewildered by all that they have learned
of our country

Our country's sinking in a whirlpool, and it's only by
The ship of learning that salvation can be earned
for our country

And if our country's daughters seek out knowledge they
Will be its mothers with the wisdom that they've learned
for our country

Woman's the soul, and man the body of our country
With soul and body linked, new life will have returned
to our country

See that our daughters raise into the sky Moses' white hand
And may a miracle in this way be confirmed[10]
for our country

And may the knotty problems that beset our country
Be undone by their nimble fingertips, concerned
for our country

Makhfi-ye Badakhshi

1876–after 1951

The daughter of the poet Mir Mahmud Shah Ajez, Makhfi-ye Badakhshi was from Faizabad, the capital of Badakhshan, the northeastern province of Afghanistan. She remained unmarried and is said to have called herself Makhfi in honor of the seventeenth-century Indian poet Makhfi (whom she referred to as "Makhfi-ye Hendi").

★

>The friendship of the world cannot be trusted
>>Its garden shows no rose without a thorn
>I saw that from Fate's camaraderie
>>Nothing but heartfelt sorrow could be born

★

>My heart, be separate from both worlds now, if you can—[11]
>Lovesick, and traveling in love's valley, be a man
>
>Be in the desert like Majnun, a prosperous king
>Forgetting obligations, home, and everything!
>
>Don't, like a nightingale, complain from every tree
>Be like the moth who, as she burns, burns silently
>
>And make your heart Majnun's, bow to it and confess
>Its sovereignty, whatever faith you might profess.
>
>Nothing will ease this pain, whatever you might do—
>The wine, the pourer, and the glass, all must be you.[12]

Farkhondeh Savoji

Late nineteenth / early twentieth century

Her father's name was Mohammad Kazem Khan, her husband's Sayf Lashkar-e Khaj. She lived near Saveh, in western Iran.

★

It's winter, and the nightingales have left
Our orchards and our gardens quite bereft.
Bring us the wine that warms the soul, my boy,
That softens hearts when sipped and brings us joy;
Pour Jamshid's wine, and Kay Kavus's, pour us[13]
Wine from the famous kings who went before us,
A drop of which makes ants imagine they
Are epic heroes ready for the fray.
Bring rose-hued wine that scours away the rust
From lovers' hearts, and cleanses them of dust.
Bring wine into the garden to revive
My weary heart that's scarcely still alive,
Bring us that fount of life—one drop will give
A hundred corpses strength enough to live,
Bring it to me, whose soul's so sad and wan
You'd say my hold on life has almost gone.
Bring me a goblet-full when nightfall comes
And bring me tambourines and harps and drums;
Bring me a glittering bowl brimful of wine
That shines as Badakhshan's bright rubies shine.[14]

Jannat
1886–1940

A granddaughter of Fath Ali Shah (r. 1797–1834), Jannat was said to have been an infant prodigy who showed her skill as a poet while still a child. She was married at the age of thirteen to Mustafa Qoli Khan Hajeb al-Doleh, who encouraged her in her poetic ambitions. Her poetry became well known in her own lifetime, and won the admiration of a number of prominent poets of the period. Many of Jannat's poems are well turned, fairly conventional poems on love or the vicissitudes of life, but she became best known for the political poem given here ("The branding of my land . . ." on p. 125).

★

My fate in life has proven, more or less,
To be to know this world's unhappiness.

Get used to grief, my heart; ignore mankind,
Since man is ignorant of manliness—

Consort with devils or with beasts, but don't
Confide in man the tale of your distress.

If enemies should hurt you, don't expect
Your friends to heal you with a kind caress—

Friends' kindness lasts a moment, and the next
They're filled with anger, spite, and bitterness.

Good faith is built on rickety foundations—
What firm foundations hold up faithlessness!

Come then, my soul, and break your body's hold,
Leave worldly men to treasure worldliness—

Seek out detachment and a private corner,
Not thrones and crowns and grandiose success.

Drink wine in memory of our ancient kings,
Drink copiously, and even to excess;

Be happy in recalling noble men
Since in man now there is no manliness.

★

If your dear friend is cruel to you, say nothing
If sorrow's arrow's pierced you through, say nothing
If you're in love, don't dare complain of sorrow,
And as for any cure for you, say nothing.

★

That one who steals all hearts, if he should have a heart,
                that wouldn't be so bad
If he should sympathize with them, and take their part,
                that wouldn't be so bad

How long my love for him has been my secret vow,
If for one moment he would share such secrets now
                that wouldn't be so bad

That man for whom I've given up this world and heaven
If he would simply give up seeing strangers even . . .
                that wouldn't be so bad

My life's gone by in missing him, in misery—
If he should somehow say he'd like to be with me
                that wouldn't be so bad

Crazy Jannat, you've mixed up poetry and prose,[15]
If he were crazier, for me, then I suppose
                that wouldn't be so bad

★

The branding of my land, its suffering and its pain,[16]
Provoke my blood and tears, dampening its soil like rain—
Its sorrow makes me long to heap earth on my head,[17]
But all its earth is gone, as if our land had fled;
Before the enemy's sharp lances must I yield
Since heartfelt tears and sighs are now my only shield?
I'll travel on along your road, and leave behind
As my bequest to you, my soul and heart and mind.[18]
O ship of hope that sinks in seas of ignorance,
I cannot look to you now for deliverance—
I sigh so much, my land, I burn, I weep, I grieve,
I have it in my mind to quit your earth, to leave
This prison where I've lost all hope, and I shall go
To tell our ancient, noble kings of what I know.
I'll say, "Our earth has gone, upon the wind it flies,
And not enough remains to make kohl for our eyes;
Where's Cyrus, Feraydun and Kay Qobad, and where[19]
Is just Anushirvan to turn to in despair?[20]
And where is Nader, so that with his saber's blows[21]
I'll root and branch destroy the source of all our foes?
The darkness of misfortune covers us with night—
I'll turn the dusk to dawn, night's darkness into light . . ."
To cut short the distress I feel, all I can do,
My country, is to sacrifice myself for you.

Kasma'i
1883–1963

Kasma'i was born in Yazd in central Iran, where her father was a merchant. She learned both Turkish and Russian, and traveled widely in Iran, Russia, and Iraq, finally settling in Tabriz in northwestern Iran, where she married and had a daughter. References in her poems indicate that she was quite well-off, and this may have been an enabling factor in the relative unconventionality of much of her life. Her travels, her seeking out of other languages and cultures than her own, and the sense of dissatisfaction expressed in her poetry—her outspoken bitterness about both women's subjection to men and Iran's subjection to the West—all indicate someone who was unusually independent for an Iranian woman of her time.

★

If I'm a member of the human race, the "noblest of creation,"
Why's my preeminence in such a wretched situation?
If I am truly human, why when strangers look at me
Do I feel flustered and ashamed at what I think they see?
What makes me differ from the splendid lord of all mankind?
The difference is he sees and hears, and I am deaf and blind;
My country isn't hidden on the moon, it's here on earth—
For all my wealth though, I depend on others for my worth.
Iran is famous in the world for her nobility—
It's this that makes me think, and gives me hope, and troubles me.

★

Even for upright men, the conscience-stricken kind,
The world of women's still an insult to the mind;
But freedom's here, deliverance's day won't wait—
Come men and women, raise your heads, don't hesitate;
What use is wringing hands and tearing clothes in fear,
The turmoil of these times will end, the day is here.

★

We who were nourished in the East, who are from the
   source of light,
Why are we far from progress now, enshrouded in
   dark night?
The West strives and exerts itself, invents the aeroplane,
And we do nothing but sit slumped in corners,
   and complain.
O splendid shining sun, why has your glorious
   radiance made
Me so withdrawn and coy, so ugly, silent, and afraid?
My nature makes me independent, and I live at ease,
Not wanting goods or wealth, just doing as I please—
It's casual contentment that's confounded us, and made us
So weak and careless that the West has conquered and
   betrayed us.

Nimtaj Salmasi

Late nineteenth / early twentieth century

Nimtaj was from Salmas in western Azerbaijan, near the border with Turkey. Apart from the fact that her father and other relatives were killed during a joint Ottoman–Kurdish raid on Salmas in 1916, virtually nothing is known about her.

★

Iranians who want their ancient monarchs' glory[22]
Must first identify the Kaveh of their story—[23]
He'll have to be a great man, his determination
Must be still greater if his strength's to save our nation;
A second Qadesiyeh's blood must run, and then[24]
Lost Andalus will hear the Moslem prayers again—[25]
An arch can't be repaired once its foundations split,
Not if a hundred times they paint and plaster it.
Our flag is men's to honor, but you rip and tear it,[26]
Then bring the tattered cloth to women to repair it,
And if they list your faults, like tousled hair combed straight,
There will be ways to solve the tangles you create.
Now in Orumiyeh the young girls openly
Go begging through the town for help and charity—
And many sisters in Salmas have put to shame[27]
Their blushing brothers who aren't worthy of the name;
We need another Noah and his floods of rain
To wash away your turpitude's disgusting stain,
And those whose constant prayer's that women should stay veiled
Should talk about their manliness, and how it's failed.
They put their trust in swords to make them free at last
But men have always done this, now and in the past.
The law was made, it must be unmade, and we'll be
Like every country that is gratified and free.

Alam Taj
1883–1947

Also known by her pen-name "Zhaleh" ("Dew"), Alam Taj was born into the wealthy Qa'em-Maqami family; she was well educated and wrote poetry from a young age. At the age of fifteen she was married to Ali Morad Khan, a military officer in his forties who was a friend of her father. The bride and groom had little in common; her husband was not interested in her poetry and forbade her to write. She continued to do so in secret, however, and hid her poems around the house, where they remained until they were discovered and published by her son after her death. Her personal poems center on her unhappy marriage and her adversarial relationship with her husband, but she also wrote a number of poems that deal more broadly with social conditions as they pertained to women; in these poems she angrily denounces what she sees as the inequities of women's status, while expressing a passionate hope that the future will bring reform and gender equality. She is sometimes referred to as Iran's first feminist poet.[28]

★

A Wish

Oh would that girls' heads wouldn't come
  Out of their mother's womb
Or if they couldn't stay there that
  They'd perish in that chamber[29]
Or that for rights denied them they
  Would dare to stretch their hands out

How sweet if women would with kindness
                Defend each others' backs
If they would plant the seeds of hope
                Within each others' hearts
If they would value who they are
                Like men in this proud country

If they'd support each other then
                Success's shoes would be there

★

This strange man who's my spouse, at least in name,[30]
Is less a husband than a leaping flame.
He's slim, dark, tall, and strong, and in my eyes
He's like a plane tree in his bulk and size;
In his dark face his eyes are sharp and bright
Like stars that glimmer on a pitch-black night;
His beard is black and white, his cheeks are thin,
And like a tiny knife inserted in
An eyeball's pupil, his sharp whiskers rasp
The skin beneath my ears; in his hands' grasp
My little body's like a dove held fast
Within a hawk's claws when it's caught at last.
How to describe his henna'd beard at night
Approaching me? It is a dreadful sight!
He's like the angel that brings death to us
Or like its phantom, pale and hideous!
He doesn't care for children or his wife
And love's of no importance in his life—

Horses and guns and money are his love,
And if he dreams they're what he's dreaming of.
He only likes one kind of poetry
And that's the *Shahnameh* of Ferdowsi;[31]
He's proud of Nader, Delhi's conqueror,[32]
And likes Rostam, invincible in war.[33]
He is an army general . . . though it's true
He has no army and no wars are due;
His fine dress uniform is just the thing
To make him feel that he's a splendid king,
He wears his sword then, and makes such a fuss . . .
To be quite honest he's ridiculous.
How ardently he longs for war, as though
He'd fight the war alone and blow by blow.
As if it were an empire still, his eyes
Behold the ancient Persian realm arise—
He is a great historian and seizes
The chance to change world history as he pleases,
Now Alexander's mighty victories,
The Arabs' conquests, are mere fantasies—
How could that Greek thief think that he'd command[34]
An army that could enter Dara's land?

For all he says, this Alexander's known
As a great prophet now, and from his throne[35]
He ruled all things on earth and in the sea,
Nothing escaped his royal sovereignty.
Then there's Vaqqas, the Arab conqueror,[36]
"Mouse eater," as men called him, who was poor,
Without a lineage and weak, who won
The crucial battle outside Ctesiphon,[37]
Because the Persian general's fatal flaw
Was even greater weakness, as he saw.

He hates the Arab people as a race,[38]
Their customs, though, he's willing to embrace;
He speaks to all so piously and well—
His secret deeds would shame an infidel.
England and Russia he sincerely hates
Along with all the European states,
He'd never know an Ottoman, although
Their cash is something that he's glad to know.
According to his faith it's fine to make
A mockery of some old bearded sheikh,
While his proud lineage is of more worth
Than all the other pedigrees on earth,
As if I had no father, whereas he
Was born into a "wealthy" family.
And he ignores the fact that in this land
My people are accustomed to command;
His ancestors were brave, but I can trace
My lineage to the Prophet's noble race.
A splendid cap is what he gets to wear
While I'm cloaked in a veil to hide my hair;
For nothing that I've done, he'll roar as loud
As if he were a bellowing thunder cloud,
And if I tell him this is not the way
To speak to women, and go on to say
A woman's gentle soul requires above
All else her children's and her husband's love,
That I love peace, and that I'm unfit for
The rowdiness of a domestic war,
He'll sneer at me and laugh . . . that spiteful laugh
Is like a knife that cuts my heart in half.

They say that once a woman is a wife
Her husband is the God that rules her life;
So he's the God of what we are . . . Ah no,
He is our sorrow and predestined woe—
What is a woman? Just a statue made
By man, the sculptor proud of his cruel trade?
If he should drive me off ? . . . he chooses to
Or hit me in his rage? . . . he's able to—
I am the woman, he's the man, I'm just
A little doll whose head's besmeared with dust.
Who am I? Oh, I'm feeble, weak, I'm one
Whom people laugh at and heap scorn upon;
Alas, in this despotic land there's no
Place where a woman can securely go.
If we say "being" and "non-being," then
Woman's "non-being," "being" is for men.
Woman's existence is her shame . . . she's frail,
Invisible, wrapped in her pitch-back veil.

★

What If

What if I'd never married, mother, how would it have been?
  What if I weren't imprisoned in my own catastrophe?
By my bad luck, I swear I wouldn't have believed the tale
  If I'd been told before that this is how my life would be.
Were my few bones so heavy then that my poor father's back
  Would have been doubled over by the unwed weight of me?
Tell me, what was I at our household's feast? A little kitten,
  Asking for what? A scrap of bread was quite enough for me.

I was a humble girl, I never asked for all the gold
   And splendid jewelry he was good enough to give to me—
If he had put me in the kitchen, like our Khosh Qadam,[39]
   I would have served as well as her in that capacity.
I bowed before your shoes, they were a crown to me, and if
   They weren't, you could have thrown them at my head, or
   poisoned me.
I thought my suitor held the Fount of Life within his hand—
   If I had not drunk down that proffered wine, how would it be?
Not just that he was old, short-tempered, mean . . . how would it be
   If we'd not married when I hadn't yet reached puberty?
If this was how I'd finish up, why was my childhood spent
   Learning my lessons, then, at this or that great savant's knee?
Why read the *Maqamat*? Why learn the *Maqulat*? And why[40]
   Tell accidence from essence with such assiduity?[41]
What profit or what harm would come to rhetoric and meaning
   If I could not explain what meaning should be logically?

★

You're in the grave now, as my father and my husband are,
   I wish that I weren't writing here all that's befallen me;
I wouldn't blame my father or reproach my mother if
   I weren't alone like this, and grieving's all that's left to me;
You're in the ground, and I am like a candle on your grave,
   Or I would not attack these ashes so insistently.
O father, mother, if you'd known what you were doing then
   I wouldn't now reproach the stars with their brutality,
And if I could be patient and accept, I would not now
   Complain of you like this, or of God's anger against me.
My dearest mother, sleep; may this familiar pain not touch you;

If I could weep, you wouldn't hear reproachful words

from me.

★

Complaining to my Samovar[42]

How comforting to me, how kind you are,
My sweetly sympathetic samovar—
As if your murmuring were a trace of wine
Within this fragile, broken cup of mine.
You burn with such peculiar unrest
You seem to share the fire within my breast;
Your eye is filled with tears, your heart with flame—
It seems that you and I are just the same
As if you learned this crying trade from me
Whose weeping eyes are wet perpetually.
How many days, how many nights, we two—
I and my mother—have sat next to you;
My sister's slender fingers fed with coal
The fire that burned within your needy soul
While dearest father—bless his memory—read
The holy scriptures once his prayers were said,
And after morning prayers were done he'd look
With care and pleasure through my homework book;
But both these angels have now spread their wings
For heaven—my wings are tattered, broken things.
My brother and my sister have both gone
Before me on that road; they've traveled on,
While in this ancient den I still remain[43]
With no one left but you to share my pain.

There is no kindly hand to clean away
The dust that lies upon my head today,[44]
No foot to guide my wasted body from
This wretched hovel to a heavenly home—
That place of meeting, love, and friendship lies
As if now washed forever from my eyes.
Like fading footprints, every memory of
My loved ones leaves me here, bereft of love.
Dear storyteller, singer of your song,
Sit down beside my bed, where you belong,
And with your gentle murmuring conspire
To splash sweet drops of water on my fire,
Since when I'm with you I'm not sad, my dear,
It gives me happiness to have you here.
I know that I'm imagining this dear friend,
And as my tale began, so it will end—
The future's yet to come, but from the past
Above my head the water's rising fast;
So sit beside me here—for now you are
My happiness, dear murmuring samovar.

★

Life's Image

1. Life

What is our life? What's seen and what is dreamed . . .
  mixed together
Comfort and pain, eagerness, weariness . . . mixed together
Pleasure, its joy, but melded with maliciousness and spite,
Gold and possessions, straining and struggle . . .
  mixed together

Hope's flicker of bright light, which is the lamp by which
　we live—
Its lovely flame, the wind that blows it out . . .
　mixed together
Truly, what's possible? What's man, who swells up with
　such pride?
A tale beset with queries by the hundred . . . mixed together
That star of the high heavens, this rotting core that is
　the earth—
Are nothing inside nothing, dreams involved with
　dreams . . . mixed together
Our every certainty hedged round with doubts and
　hesitations
Our every cause a mass of possibilities . . . mixed together
Are you aware what death is? It's a lesson learned in anguish,
A silence squabbled over endlessly . . . mixed together
The blessings of the afterlife are dreams spun out of dreams,
Earth's glory is the sun's rise, and its setting . . .
　mixed together

2. *Woman*

What is a woman, then? O God . . .! This player, plaything,
　essence
With no substance, what is she? Potshards and dirt . . .
　mixed together
Her life's years dragging on, her mind's new growth that
　comes too late,
Seeing what's here, longing for what might be . . .
　mixed together
The scalding fire that is her tears, the blaze of her deceit,
Her chastity, and her immoderate lust . . . mixed together
An artificial face, made up of eye-shadow and rouge,

A dreadful sight, the leering of a pimp . . . mixed together
An evil nature that is covered over with false beauty
A weak soul hidden with a brazen lie . . . mixed together

3. *Man*

And what is man? This empty show, this nothingness,
  this vegetable—
As though, to make him, heaven took dirt and sin . . .
  mixed together
He lifts the great flag of his manly glory to the skies
But woman's insight sees right through that flag . . . they're
  mixed together
What's man but one who scrapes a nasty morsel for
  himself—
His wife's tears and her blood have made that
  morsel . . . mixed together
His blazing love is soon extinguished in the sheets—
  he's present
But he's absent; he's kind, and then he's angry . . .
  mixed together

And what's religious marriage in our irreligious age?
It's what's unlawful and what's lawful now . . .
  mixed together
It's wedding candles that were lit with an untruthful hand
It's wedding candies cooked with mortal poison . . .
  mixed together
Is this religious marriage, or religious fornication?
But no, I'm wrong, it's marriage and it's torture . . .
  mixed together
The thing I've understood from my ill-omened marriage is
Companionship came with calamity . . . mixed together

Man is the more deceitful one, woman's the more unfaithful,
One's bad, the other's worse, and both are evil . . .
  mixed together
If one of them should turn out to be good (which happens
  rarely)
That person's filthy earth and limpid water . . .
  mixed together
Let me sum up: if someone sees existence as it is,
This world is ugly, with a bit of beauty . . . mixed together.

Zinat Amin

Late nineteenth / early twentieth century

Nothing is known about this poet except that she was still a schoolgirl when she stepped forward and recited the poem given here at a demonstration outside the Majles (parliament building) in 1908. The "Russian enemies" were the Cossack troops (a mainly Russian force in the pay of the Persian monarchy), under Colonel Liakhov, sent by Mohammad Ali Shah Qajar (r. 1907–9) to bombard the Majles and put an end to demands for constitutional reform. Like a number of poems by women written during this period, Zinat Amin's poem is as much a reproach to Iranian men as a call for political reform and a rejection of foreign interference in Iran's domestic affairs.

*

Sons of vile fathers, death is better than
A life that's lived unworthy of a man—
A wasted life does not deserve life's name,
It's a disgrace, synonymous with shame.
Your bodies do not feel our pain—where then,
Is all the manliness that makes you men?
A wretched body without zeal is worth
Less than an impure clod of senseless earth;
What honorable heart would shake with fear
As soon as Russian enemies appear?
This is a time for man's self-sacrifice,
Not shilly-shallying and cowardice!

To cower when danger threatens is to be
A byword for disgrace and infamy,
So let us fight like lions, like heroes wage
This war, and be the wonders of the age!
It's time to show your fervor, to defend
Our land with Islam as our faith and friend.

Batul Adib Soltani
1896–1993

Batul Adib Soltani came from a wealthy middle-class family; her father was an amateur poet and an older brother wrote newspaper articles in support of the Constitutional Revolution of 1905–11. Her husband, who worked in the Ministry of Education, was a great lover of poetry and enthusiastically encouraged his wife's poetic ambitions. She published three books of poetry, and continued to write verse into her eighties.

★

In this tumultuous world my hope was I
Would not be one of those who cheat and lie,
I hoped the jewelry I would wear would be
The rings of virtue and sincerity,
I hoped I'd rein my stubborn nature in
By practice and by arduous discipline,
I hoped I'd keep my page of Being clean
From everything nefarious or mean,
I hoped I'd use my gift of poetry
Only for praising someone dear to me;
But Fate had other things for me to do—
I could not shun the things I wanted to.

Parvin Etesami
1907–41

Parvin Etesami was born in Tabriz in northwestern Iran, but grew up in Tehran where she attended an American school for girls. After graduation she briefly taught at the school. While she was still an adolescent, her poetry attracted favorable attention, particularly from the poet laureate Malek al-Shoara Bahar. In 1934 she married a relative of her father's, but the marriage lasted for only ten weeks, and after it ended she is said never to have mentioned it or her husband again. She was an intensely private person and had a reputation for extreme shyness; she was asked to become a tutor at the Pahlavi court but refused to do so, and when later in life she became relatively well known for her poetry she almost always refused to give interviews. She died of typhoid fever at the age of thirty-four. Parvin Etesami is the last major woman poet to write wholly within the conventions of pre-modern Persian poetry, and she is often referred to as the greatest of women poets to have written in that tradition.[45]

★

My rose, what did you see among flowers, in the garden,
Apart from scolding, spiteful thorns, what did you see?
In the bazaar, my ruby, shining with such radiance,
Apart from that mean customer, what did you see?
You went into the fields, your fate was to be caged,
Apart from this cage, captured bird, what did you see?[46]

★

An Orphan's Tears

A king passed by, and cheering from the crowd
On rooftops and in streets rang long and loud;
A little orphan there asked, "What's that thing
That's shining on the crown worn by the king?"
And someone answered him, "What's that? Who knows?
A splendid priceless gemstone, I suppose."
A hunchbacked crone came forward and replied,
"That stone is blood you've shed, and tears we've cried;
For years this wolf has fleeced his flock, and look,
We're fobbed off with the shepherd's rags and crook—
The king who steals his subjects' wealth's no better
Than some cruel cut-throat or a wretched beggar!
Look at an orphan's falling tears aright
To see what makes that royal jewel so bright."
     Parvin, what use are righteous words to those
      Whose thoughts are twisted and whose minds are
                  closed?

★

White and Black[47]

A white dove, as dawn broke, prepared to fly
Up from her nest into the morning sky,
An arrow struck her as she sought to rise . . .
The aftermath of this was no surprise:
Her wings were wounded, hope's thread snapped, each vein
Seemed split apart by an atrocious pain.
A black crow passed her nest, and grew alarmed

To see how grievously the dove was harmed.
He stopped to care for her, and dexterously
He built from thorns and straw a canopy
To shield her from the sun's glare, and did all
He could to make his patient comfortable,
Straining and struggling, weaving leaves to make
A dense green curtain for the sufferer's sake;
He brought her water in his beak, and then
Delicious fruit to make her well again—
He was her parents, her brave adjutant,
Her comfort, caretaker, and confidant.
The dove had had a wretched time of it
But now her pain relented, bit by bit.
The dove asked, "What have black and white to do
With one another? Who persuaded you
To make friends with a stranger in this way?"
The crow replied, "Well yes, it's as you say,
We're different colors, but we're one inside—
Between your needs and mine there's no divide.
Like me, you have a heart in you, and love,
Like you, I've veins and blood in me, dear dove.
We should be honest, of one heart, and true,
Friendship is always friendship, old or new."
    When we see others suffering we should stay
    And do what must be done, not walk away;
    Good will's the key to happiness, we're told,
    Whether it's made of iron or of gold.

*

A preacher asked his son once if he knew
What Islam is, what Moslems ought to do—
"It's truthfulness, my child, it's being kind,
It's helping others, it's a gentle mind,
It's prayerfulness, sincere humility—
To all of life, my child, it is the key."
The boy replied, "By this criterion,
In our town, father, there is only one
True Moslem here—he's an Armenian."[48]

★

Once women in Iran were not Iranians you'd say;[49]
They lived bewildered and in darkness then from day to day,
Their lives and deaths took place in corners, in obscurity.
What were they in those days, but prisoners held perpetually?
No one has lived through such dark centuries as women have
Or been betrayed by faith's hypocrisies as women have—
In law courts women had no witnesses to state their case,
In schools of excellence and knowledge women had no place,
Women who wanted justice then could wait their whole life
    through
Unanswered . . . this was obvious, not something no one knew;
Many there were who wore the kindly shepherd's cloak, but
    they
Weren't kindly shepherds, they were wolves that saw us as their
    prey.
For women, life's wide, splendid playing field was nothing more
Than that small corner of the field that they were fated for,
Men made sure knowledge was a light that women didn't see,
Their ignorance was not from dullness or stupidity—
How can a woman stitch if she's denied the thread to sew?

How can she reap a harvest when she has no fields to sow?
The fruits of knowledge overflow the vendor's piled-high stall
But women's share of them has always been no fruit at all.
This bird has lived her life out in a cage, and there she dies
And gardens never hear of her, for there she never flies,
Her fate's obedience, which is a desert and a pit,
Because what way can she pursue and not be hurt by it?

It is the glow and hue of knowledge that we need—they are
Finer than ruby red or emerald necklaces by far,
A hundred silks cannot compare with one plain simple dress—
Honor derives from worth, not self-indulgent silliness,
The wearer gives her clothes and shoes their worth; price is no
   guide
To how corrupt or principled the wearer is inside.
Simplicity and purity are jewels, so let them shine—
Their glorious luster shouldn't skulk unnoticed in a mine,
What use are gold and jewelry when a woman has no sense,
Since ignorance can't hide behind her tawdry ornaments?
Faults should be clothed in chastity, and in no other dress—
Flamboyant and flirtatious clothes are just like nakedness,
But if a woman's chaste and serious, she can be sure
No kind of dress can harm the reputation of the pure.
A woman's like a treasury whose thieves are lust and greed
And woe to her if she is not the sentinel they need;
The devil's not a guest who dines with virtue—he's aware
That if he turned up for a meal he'd be unwelcome there.

The road of righteousness must be our road, since if we stray
Regret's the only food we'll find to eat along the way;
The eyes and heart must be kept back, but Islam doesn't mean
That piety's a wretched veil ensuring we're not seen.

Empty-Handed

A little girl went to a party where
She tried to join some girls already there;
One frowned at her, and one was quick to snatch
Her own skirt back, one pointed out a patch
Sewn on the new girl's knee, one mocked her dress,
One said her hair was an atrocious mess,
One said she was too pale . . . their victim heard
What they were saying, every whispered word.

She said, "You laugh at me; the heavens too
Have sniggered at my poverty, like you;
My heart's been hurt, but this is how I live,
And I put up with what the heavens give.
Why should I care what other people say
When life has treated me in this cruel way?
You've no idea of what I struggle through—
The snake of bad luck hasn't bitten you.
The rich have dressmakers, but poverty,
Who is my seamstress, cut these clothes for me.
My mother washed her hands of life, she's gone;
Without her hand to bless me I live on.
My fingers comb my hair, no one at home
Has ever thought of buying me a comb;
This morning brushwood scratched my hands, the red[50]
Blotch on my dress is where the scratches bled.
I've had a bitter time of it, but we
Must drink the wine fate hands to you and me.
Games children play are pleasant, but my name
Was never chosen for a children's game—

What is a childhood when the child can't run
Or laugh or leap or join in any fun?
The wind of poverty is cold and raw
And always leaves me trembling like a straw—
In every task I thought that I'd complete
The thread snapped, and lay tangled at my feet.[51]
Luck's stream is milk, they say; when I went there
To drink from it, blood was my scalding share;[52]
There are a hundred ways, with every breath,
A poor unhappy person meets with death,
And yet she can't escape from being here,
Her life, that's made of misery and fear.
The eyes see things, and no one said to me
That there are some things that I shouldn't see . . .
My red shoes faded, my green bracelet broke,
When New Year comes it's usual for folk
To have new clothes, but I have none to show,[53]
On New Year's Eve it's usual to go
To bath-houses with friends, but I have none,
I can't afford it and have never gone.
My life is like a branch that storms assail,
That lightning blasts, that's beaten down by hail;
The pages of my life are black as night
And not a single one of them is white.
The farmer of the stars has sown the field
That is our life, we reap what it will yield
Of thorns or flowers; as heaven has done before
It makes one rich and strong, another poor;
You haven't run from me, and I'm surprised—
Poor folk like me are usually despised.
Children are fond of songs and novelties
But I can't offer you delights like these—
The door of happiness stays shut for me,

Whoever locked it threw away the key,
And since to me Good Fortune's veiled her face,
I don't belong here with you, in this place.
Oh I was rich last night, before I slept,
My wealth was all the glistening pearls I wept;
Would that I'd stored my mother's kisses when
She used to kiss me, to be felt again
Upon my face that's now kissed only by
The trickling of my teardrops when I cry.
Lucky the child whose mother's here to bless
Her little girl with constant happiness;
My mother was my only jewel, but she
Was stolen by the world's black crow from me."[54]

★

Night

Evening approaches, and the stars' faint light
Above the garden glitters in the night.
Night's leopard leaves its ambush and draws near,
And day's gazelle conceals herself in fear.
As he turns homeward, tired in every limb,
The woodman's load weighs heavily on him;
Exhausted by his work of dragging seeds
The tired ant too seeks out the rest he needs,
And as has happened since the days of old
The shepherd leads his flock back to its fold;
Doves fill their dovecots now, to sleep and rest,
Kites leave off scavenging to seek their nest.

The world's in mourning . . . like a mourner's cry
An owl's call echoes in the evening sky;
The hens are roosting, millet seeds lie round,
Unpecked yet, scattered on the trampled ground.
A laborer lays his tools down, since it's late
And his unfinished task will have to wait.
The snake-charmer's asleep, as is his snake,
And neither smith nor smithy are awake.
An old dear's blanket's torn, but her weak sight
Can't see to thread her needle now it's night.
Even trapped prey's at rest, as if the day
Had dawned, and it could simply slip away.
The reaper props his idle scythe upon
His shoulder now his daily work is done,
The forester at home in bed pulls all
His covers round him to be comfortable.
But the appointed watchman stays awake—
It's good he does so, for the sleepers' sake!
On rooftops thieves are moving now it's late,
On highways hidden robbers watch and wait;
A sick man grumbles he can't sleep, his dread
Is that a painful, sleepless night's ahead.
The sheep have all been milked, and resting now
The oxen lie unyoked beside their plough;
Shouts ring out from a bar, and there's the sound
Of glasses smashing as the drinks go round.
The dark is like the earth's shield, as if black
Could be chainmail against the stars' attack;
There in the east, Venus begins to shine,
A jewel translucent in a pitch-black mine,
A shooting star streaks briefly through the dark
As though a slingshot's pebble struck its mark.

Like oozing blood, the stars of the Great Bear
Turn red, as though a mourner tore her hair,
The still stars seem to stare, as convicts hear
Their sentence, and remain transfixed with fear.
Through chinks, in shanties of the poor, the pale
Moon's light grows dim, and as it starts to fail
Dawn breaks . . . the sun's now like a houri who
Escapes from Ahriman, and shines anew.[55]
Dews wash the hyacinth's tight curls, and clean
The dirt from lily-of-the-valley's sheen;
Once more the ant's long labors are renewed,
And sparrows start to peck about for food.

Some days are like a placid horse; some rear
And buck and plunge, this way and that they veer;
As Fate has always been, so it will be—
Time is our friend, and then our enemy,
It's day, then night, its revolutions bring
December's snows to us, and then the spring.
The caravan of life moves surely on
And leaves us grieving for the time that's gone;
Born to unrest, caught in an evil snare,
None can escape this world of harsh despair—
Whether your state is good or bad, no force
Will modify the world's incessant course.
My friend, there's silk upon this merchant's stall,
At times . . . at times there's burlap and that's all!
Polish the mirror of your soul, you must,[56]
Scour it with knowledge of corrosive rust.
Don't be ungrateful; in the wilderness
God fed the Jews, and pitied their distress.
You read these books of wise theology

And yet you hardly know your ABC!
                    Why are you so afraid, Parvin? Just say
                    The truth; truth's not a thing to hide away.

                              ★

Sorrow and Poverty

A woman bent beside her spindle said,
"From spinning you, I've white hairs on my head,
My eyes grow dark, my poor back gives me trouble,
It's hard for me to see and I'm bent double,
Clouds gather over me, they weep and say
My winter's here . . . That winter's borne away
My friends like falling leaves—I'm left alone,
There's nothing here that I can call my own.
Charcoal and wood are things that I can't pay for
And they're the only things I hope and pray for.
Each little bird is snug now in its nest
And even insects scuttle off to rest.
Now the sun's set, what light will there be for
Those who must work at night because they're poor?
From darning tears and mending holes, blood seeps
Beneath my nails, and it's my heart that weeps.
There's not an unpatched part of what I wear,
As one bit's sewn, another patch will tear;
My hands were trembling and there wasn't light
For me to thread my needle by last night,
And then I smelled my neighbor's meal, and crept
Hungry to bed, and hungrily I slept.
When I see clouds or rain, my heart beats fast,

Wondering how long my leaky roof will last,
With all the snow and mud how could I mend it?
And I'm afraid that one more storm will end it.
Instead of curtains when I wake I see
The ceiling webs the spiders weave for me,
And when I walk to see new flowers, I meet
At every step with thorns that pierce my feet,
I've seen such floods of awful things, believe me,
And I've wept floods of tears for things that grieve me."

      Why is it those with wealth and power ignore
      The dreadful sufferings of their country's poor?
      Parvin, the wealthy have no sympathy
      For the impoverished and their misery—
      How many times is it that you've been told
      It's useless to beat iron that's grown cold?

Zhaleh Esfahani

1921–2007

She was born in Esfahan. Despite her father's disapproval, her mother insisted that she go to school; at first she attended a local elementary school run by British missionaries, and then a high school in Tehran. As a young woman, she became ideal-istically involved in leftist politics, which in Iran at that time were dominated by the Soviet Union. In 1943 she married a member of Iran's Tudeh (communist) party; her husband was briefly imprisoned for his political activism, and on his release in 1947 the couple fled from Iran, moving first to Baku and later to Moscow. She stayed in the Soviet Union until the Iranian Islamic Revolution of 1979, when she returned to Iran. Two years later, disillusioned with the policies of the Islamic Republic's theocratic government, she moved to England, where she remained until her death. She wrote poetry throughout her life, from childhood until old age; much of it was political in nature, but she also had a strong lyric gift, and this is apparent in even her most ideological work.[57]

★

Forest and River[58]

> The forest cried out to the river:
> I wish I were like you
> Traveling day and night, with such sights to see,
> Down to the limpid, open sea

A riverbed of shining water
A restless eager soul
A surging, turquoise-colored light
Flowing forever

And what am I?
A captive caught in earth
In eternal silence
I'll grow old
I'll turn yellow
I'll dry up
I'll be a handful of cold ashes
Sooner or later

The river shouted:
Forest, you're half awake
I wish I were in your place
That I knew such lucid, emerald peace
On glittering moonlit nights,
To be the mirror in which spring sees herself
The spreading shade where lovers meet

Your destiny's to be renewed each year
And mine's to abscond from myself
All I know is to run in confusion

                                    to run
                                          and run
From all this migrating and journeying
What do I get
                    except futility and restlessness?
Ah not for a moment is my soul ever at peace!

No one knows
                    another's heart
Who can say of a passer-by
                    who he is or was?

A man walks in shadow, asking himself under his breath,
Who am I?
River?
Forest?
Both together?
Forest and river?
Forest and river.

★

When I depart this wretched world, be sure
To burn my corpse to ashes, and what's more
See that my ashes come to rest in water
And scatter them at sea, not in a river.
I want to sing together with the sea,
One with its soul and its immensity,
Sing songs that call up mighty storms, the crash
Of tumbling waves, the lightning's sudden flash,
Songs of the ocean's joy, its light flung wide,
Songs brimful with its passion and its pride.

When I depart this wretched world, be sure,
O God, to vex and bother me no more,
Since on this earth I've borne enough from You,
Trapped here and made to suffer all You do.
I've written this while on a moving train,
As restless as the thoughts within my brain;
I and my couplets, we'll both carry on,
Old-fashioned now—tomorrow we'll be gone.

When I depart this wretched world, be sure
I'll tell the chamberlain who guards hell's door,
"I'm just like fire, I'm heathen, you can't turn me,
I'm a poet, a poet—you'd better burn me;
I didn't want the world's filth, fit for curses,
I gave it something beautiful—my verses."

I've written this while on a moving train
To make sure nothing of it will remain.

★

Where Am I from, You Want to Know

Where am I from, you want to know
I'm a gypsy, one who'll come and go
Raised in pain and sorrow

Look at a map of the world, the whole expanse,
Cross all the countries' borders at a glance

It's certain you won't find a single country where
There's no one from my country there,
Living hand to mouth

My soul's in turmoil and I fall asleep
Moonlit nights; deep
In the world of sleep
I wander over endless boulders of my longing

By asking where I'm from
You've woken me from all
That golden dream; I've fallen from the high roof of my
    longing
To the foot of reality's wall

Where am I from, you want to know
From a country that's rich and poor
From the green foothills of the Alborz[60]
From the shores of the wonderful Zayandeh Rud River[61]
And from Persepolis's ancient palaces

Where am I from, you want to know
From a land of poetry and love and the sun
From a country of conflict and hope and oppression
From the barricades of revolution's victims
My eyes are burning, thirstily waiting—
Now do you know
Where I'm from?

*

Return

The alleyway's the same alleyway, the city the same city,
the mountain that same mountainside, the stream that
  same stream,
the trees in the same place, Zendeh Rud in the same
  place,[62]
the beautiful domes, the minarets and their summits,
the eternal epic as it was

On the walls and doors a thousand slogans
the city's been busy since the revolution
the city of artists, industry, and warfare
a city preoccupied with poverty and great wealth
the smiling of turquoise, the dancing of gold
on the shop doors, in the hubbub of the bazaar
fresher than gardens on spring mornings
carpets that show gardens, cloth printed from wood-blocks
so much fruit at the side of the street, in the square
the wide, staring eyes of hungry children
the heart-wrenching scent of newly baked bread
the Zayandeh Rud's bank with its press of young people
here's news from the front, here's news of the war[63]
Oh to wipe out that war's spirit and name
cursed by so much blood and destruction
once again lamps will be lit commemorating the fallen
in windows, in shops, at the roadside
on one side this ruinous war's refugees
on the other men committed to war
on their way to defend the homeland, rifles sloped on
  shoulders,
determined and stubborn and angry and silent

The layout of a city filled with magic, the glitter of moonlight
the river the same river, and the river water not that water
the city's sweet young girl, where has she gone?
has she burned, become smoke, the smoke gone into air?
or like a bird has she flown the nest,
gone, never to see the nest again?
or after long years of flight
has she now returned to her nest

I wander the streets, go from house to house
looking everywhere for the one I lost
they say she was the one who made our hearts happy,
the shadow of the young girl is everywhere
on that mountain top, sometimes by this river,
she's running, scurrying here and there,
on she goes, looking for tomorrow

Sweet young girl of this city, where are you?
appear now, we're two friends, we know each other
we're companions, with the same soul, the same voice
your red cheeks have become my wrinkled face
my life and yours devoted to our country
oh how happy and proud I am that we have done this!

In the time of plunder and the crown, the sly
    nightwatchman
wanted me to return and be like a slave[64]
in my country to be wretched and humble
I didn't listen to his dangerous words
so that I wouldn't turn to smoke, the smoke from his flames
the ache for my country remained, and my conscience's
    honor,
clear-sighted, with a heart filled with longing—

though all my life was spent harried by traveling
I'll never say my life's gone by in vain

So, off you go my sweet girl, and may God keep you!
who am I saying "go" to?
it's a long time since you went
and never returned

Oh youth, the young shoot blossoming
in my sons who are my fruit,
you've gone, and I go; what's there to be sorry for?
all these young souls are as my soul was
this is how it was since time began
the young shoot giving blossoms and fruit

Once again myself, and Esfahan's clear sky
all these shining eyes filled with anticipation
this was my wish, to see my friends and my homeland
I'm grateful that I stayed alive, that I've seen them,
that my wish was fulfilled, even though it's so late.
Here is the beginning of my being and of my poetry
the growing and blossoming
of my sapling of hope.

Simin Behbahani
1927–2014

Simin Behbahani's father was a poet, journalist, and newspaper editor, and her mother was a teacher of French; she too worked as a newspaper editor for a while, and both parents were active in patriotic and reformist politics. As a child, Behbahani grew up in a household steeped in both literature and political activism, and also one in which the value of women's intellectual lives was taken for granted. Given this background it is not surprising that she began to write poetry while still very young, and that she remained involved in reformist politics throughout her life. Her poetry uses both traditional and modernist techniques, and covers a very wide range of subjects, from the intimately personal to poems on social questions of general concern. She is regarded as one of the greatest of Iran's twentieth-century writers and was twice nominated for the Nobel Prize. She was twice married and had two sons. Toward the end of her life, she fell foul of the Islamic Republic's government and was forcibly prevented from leaving Iran in 2010, when she was eighty-two and almost blind. She died five years later, in Tehran, and many thousands of mourners are said to have attended her funeral.[65]

★

Prostitute's Song

Give me that pot of rouge
I'll put some color on my colorless flesh
Give me that cream, I'll make my careworn
Wrinkled face look young and fresh

Give me that musky perfume and I'll scent
My hair spread on my shoulders; pass me
My tight dress, so that in their arms
They'll tightly clasp me.

Give me that chiffon whose see-through sheen
Doubles the lure of nakedness—
That goads their lust and makes them want
My body and my breasts

Give me that wine glass, so I'll get drunk
And laugh at my dark fate a while
So that my worn, unhappy face will show
A cheerfully deceiving smile

Oh God, last night's companion
Was so exasperating, such a loser . . . but I
 Could only say when he asked how it was,
"I've never met a more attractive guy"

As for that "husband" of the night before
The one who made me ill
If he'd paid me a hundred times what he paid
Pain would have made me sicker still.

Too many people round me, and I've no one—
No friends to be supportive, or to care,
How they protest how much they care for me—
A moment later they're not there

No husband who would share my pillow
Whose faithful hand would guard me, who'd be kind,
No child, no dearest one who would
Scour clean this rust that tarnishes my mind

And oh, who's that, who's banging there?
My "husband" for tonight is at the door;
O sorrow, leave my heart alone; it's time
To give him what he's come here for.

O lips, my lips that sell deceit,
Veil your sad secrets now and smile,
And so they'll leave a few more coins for me
Kiss them, flirt with them, use all your guile . . .

★

Dancing Girl

The dancing girl was about to dance—from the heart
Of the bar there erupted a deafening shout;
She shook her blonde hair free, her pleated skirt twirled,
From the hearts of the drunks a wild cry burst out

The sound of the music, the clinking of glasses,
Bursts of laughter and yelling, all mixed in confusion—

Twisting and turning, the curved wave of her body,
Enticing the audience to fiery abandon

A trembling of joy in the flesh of the drunks
As her bared breasts like ivory started to shake,
The glitter of sequins on the silk of her skirt
Was like sunlight at dawn on the waves of a lake

Her waist like a snake that twisted with hunger
As slippery as mercury, as smooth and as bright,
A glimpse of her thigh through the slit in her skirt
Was a flash of the moon from the depths of the night

The dance came to an end, the wine-lovers clapped,
They tore at their clothes till they hung there in strands,
They threw flowers on the head of the flower that had opened,
And bit in their pleasure the backs of their hands[66]

But the dancing girl, just as she hadn't the evening before,
Didn't smile, wasn't happy, took no cute curtain call—
Instead her face frowned, she made fists of her hands,
The joy of her lovers didn't please her at all

Her eyes they were feverish, and heavy with languor,
Her drunkenness showed both her pain and regret
The wine in her mind was burning and fiery, she longed
For a life filled with joy, which she'd never known yet

For all of her life she'd given others such pleasure
But pleasure had never been why her heart raced,
All her life she'd served others the wine of delight
While she'd had not a drop of it, not even a taste

And so that her crying wouldn't make sorrow worse,
She hid her charred feelings, her lips were sealed tight,
Like a candle she was, whose flame was her longing,
Dancing for others, burning down through the night

Oh how she felt she must have her heart's justice
And wrest all its grief from the mob in this lair
Then perhaps she'd escape from this sickening hell-hole,
Free her feet from the chains that were holding her there

Loudly she shouted, "You louts who abuse me,
Don't throw me a flower and don't blow me a kiss—
You've broken my back with this burden of pain
And I thirst for your blood—yes it's me who says this!"

Then one of the crowd cried, "The girl's drunk, and tonight
She's gone far too far, it's the drinks that she's had;
But look how her anger has turned her face black—
It's not drink that has done this, the poor thing's gone mad!"

Again the girl shouted, "Just which of you, tell me,
Which one of the lot of you, tell me, which one
Tomorrow won't reproach himself knowing
My youth faded like this until it was gone?

"Which of you? Tell me! Who's there among you
Who'll free me from all of the drunks gathered here?
Who'll put all my life back in order, take my hand,
And make the road I should travel appear?"

Among the drunks the girl's words produced silence
A strange pause in the noise, a dead quiet—and after
This moment of silence the crowd gave its answer . . .
A few scattered bursts of contemptuous laughter

★

The End of Waiting

I have a thousand hopes, and all of them are you
The start of happiness, the end of waiting's you

Those past springs that I lived through without you,
What were they then but autumns, since the spring is you?

My heart is empty now of everything but you
So stay still where you are, be permanent and true

A shooting star's a matter of impulsive moments
The star that mocks the darkness of the night is you

If all the people in the world desire my blood
What should I be afraid of? My loving friend is you

My heart's a jug that's overflowing with desire
I have a thousand hopes, and all of them are you

★

Gone from my heart, from my arms, from my memory,
Don't look at me, I cannot bear your gaze
Don't look at me, because your black eyes
Have left only bitter sadness in my memory

Gone from my heart, so tell me, truly, why
You've come back to me tonight
If you've come for that lover you desired
I'm not her, she is dead and I am her shadow

I'm not her, no, my heart is cold and black
Her melancholy heart had sparks of love within it
Everywhere, with everyone, whatever happened,
She longed for you, my faithless love

I'm not her, my eyes are dull and dumb
Her eyes contained so many hidden words
And that sad love in those dark eyes like night
Was more mysterious than twilight in the evenings.

No, I'm not her, it's a long time since
These colorless lips blossomed because of your love
But there were always life-giving smiles on her lips
Sleeping like moonlight on dewy flowers

Don't look at me, I cannot bear your gaze,
That person you want from me, I swear she's dead
She was in my body and suddenly I don't know
How she saw, or what she did, or where she went, or
  why she died

I am her grave, I am her grave, on her warm body
I placed the cold camphor of regret
She died, and in my breast this pitiless heart
Is the stone that I placed on that grave.

★

For What?

For what? That I stay for two hundred years
looking at cruelty and corruption,
that I see each day through to its end
each night through till dawn,
that each dawn from behind the window
I see the mocking face of the sun
and look at another day
with immense disgust
before bitter tea has touched my lips
then once again the writhing squirming struggle . . .
that I go over the tale once again
of the book of Balkh's poet[67]
a cage, the whole world a cage, a cage
I think of fleeing
of pulling my cloak round my body
my head scarf over my hair . . .
to the streets of nowhere.
In the midst of depravity and misery, in this smoke,
this sorrow for all that is and is not
I begin my complaint against oppression.
Although you've called me again
all our friends are suffering
shall I leave them in the midst of disaster?
For what? That I enjoy myself again
For what? That your good doctors
make me well again
and I take the risk, suitcase in hand
that I'm ready to travel again
that I come, and my heart is renewed
that I come with my eyes unclouded[68]

that I come and among your people
I once again make a stir with my poems
But I haven't fallen into this snowy cloud
in such a way that I'll get out again
I don't imagine I'll reach safety, that I'll emerge
from this profound disaster.
My old friend, dear friend,
leave me in this dream of winter—
it's possible, who knows,
that I can soothe my soul and body.
If a gentle spring breeze
bringing the green of new growth
should waft across my dried-up nerves
my body might bear fruit.

★

We weep honey
we smile poison[69]
We're content to be miserable
we're miserably content
We've washed our hands in blood
we've washed blood from our hands
And nothing came of either
as we weep we smile
It was eight years, but
we didn't know what it meant
Children in a line, we knew nothing
of how and why
In the garden, like a storm,
we snapped off every twig
From the vine's chandelier
we broke off each bunch of grapes
If the tree flourished
it was a stubborn tree
We broke its branches,
tore up its roots
Longing for war
we brought on disaster
Now, regretting what we've done
we long for peace
We broke from their bodies
heads and wings
Looking to put things right
we're busy grafting

Will it fly
will it live
This wing we sew back on
this head we're tying on?

Lobat Vala
Born 1930

Born in Tehran, Lobat Vala was associated as a young poet with both Simin Behbahani (p. 164) and Forugh Farrokhzad (p. 179). Her poetry achieved wide popularity when she was still young, and a number of her poems were used as lyrics for popular songs. She found herself profoundly out of sympathy with the social policies of the Islamic Republic established in 1979, and in 1980 moved to Melbourne, Australia, where she lived from 1980 to 1984; she earned an MA in Middle Eastern Studies from the University of Melbourne. In 1984 she moved to London, where she now lives.[70]

★

Footprint

I went to see him the next morning
My cheeks bright red with last night's shame
Telling myself tales of need and passion—
His gaze was a devilish flame

I'd words of apology on my lips
Embarrassment made my heart beat faster
My flesh was a sore inflamed with sadness
My chest hid a seething disaster

Quietly I said, "Can I ask you
To erase my image from your mind?
The event that happened between us,
Please let it disperse on the wind."

His gaze burned my eyes; that stolen kiss
Made his passion, like a flower, expand—
He smiled at my tears so kindly
And touched his lips then with his hand,

"There is a gentle footprint here
Left by the kiss we can't reclaim—
My caravan of grief has gone,
It's been replaced by passion's flame;

"I can't forget you while my lips
Still bear that kiss's burning trace
And even though the passion fades
Still I'll be lost in your embrace."

Ah me! Would that I could forever
Brand him into my memory—
But down the days' long road love fled,
No trace of it remains in me.[71]

*

That friend who boasted of his pure sincerity
Had nothing in his purse but rank hypocrisy,
My hair's turned white, but even so I was naïve
Enough to tell myself he really wanted me.

*

Old and tired and silent
my shoulders weighed down with grief and care
far from my country and friends
impatient, in despair
I wait
in a dream's quiet solitude,
broken winged, my soul grown faint,
on the black screen of my fearful mind I paint
the color of light
I draw flowers and fruit—
the memory of childhood's streets
the memory of green years.
The years of folly and craziness
won't leave my mind,
the dream of good memories, regret
for past happiness, days with no sunset,
they'll never leave my mind.
My city that has no spring,
in mourning for light
with night's black veil drawn over its head . . .
I cannot believe that the backs of my dreamed-of heroes
are bent beneath this weight of sorrow
I cannot believe it—
the skies of my city were not so grief-stricken!
My head whirls with this question:
Who stole the sun from my house?
How did a devil of darkness manage this deed?
Is it that kindness is asleep?

From within a mirror—
apart from which there's nothing left
that speaks my language, feels as I do—
dread strikes me:
"That deceitful, shameless filth,
the one who stole the sun
from the sky above your house, was no one
but you."

★

Reed-bed

I'm going to teach fish
How to live among reeds,
Just as a bird that feeds
On fish once taught me how
To live among slime and weeds.

★

Still Young

My glass still holds a drop of wine
My mouth knows sweet and bitter as still mine
I drink the wine still from the vat of our existence
Still hear dawn's chirping chorus in the distance
On water still see moonlight's splendor glint
Still on the breeze catch rose and pennyroyal's scent
My body's fire still burns within my memory
My sense of touch is still with me

I wait for spring still, still plant seeds,
Still follow where light leads . . .
Still I'm in love with tales that rouse and stir us
And still with hope sing every song and chorus
My poetry still seeks for love
And still—if wearily and lamely now—
I hope to see the Simorgh[72]
Upward I go, toward the peak,
Still longing for the Friend I seek
Still . . .
Come then, and smash my mirror against sorrow's stone
Look! I'm still young

Forugh Farrokhzad
1934–67

Forugh Farrokhzad's father was a military officer, and seems to have had little sympathy with his daughter's artistic ambitions. In 1951, at the age of sixteen, she fell in love with the satirist Parviz Shapour, married. and gave birth to a son (Kamyar) a year later. She was divorced from her husband in 1954, and lost custody of Kamyar. In 1958 she began a relationship with the writer and film-maker Ebrahim Golestan, which lasted until her death in a car crash at the age of thirty-two. Her poetry's technical innovations, as well as their sexually explicit frankness about women's inner lives, made her notorious in her own lifetime; her writings won her many admirers and imitators, and have made her the best-known Iranian Persian-language woman poet of the twentieth century both within Iran and outside of it. She made a highly respected documentary film, *The House Is Black*, in 1962 about a leper colony in Azerbaijan; while working on this film she adopted the son of two of the colony's inhabitants.[73]

★

Captive[74]

> I want you, and I know my heart's desire,
> To hold you in my arms, will never come to me;
> You are the sky that's clear and bright—and I'm
> A captive bird, a cage's corner's home to me
>
> And from these cold gray bars I gaze
> With longing and with wonder at your face;

I think that help will come, and that I'll spread
My wings, and fly toward you from this place

I think that in a moment when the jailer's careless
From this silent cell I'll fly up and be free
And I shall laugh then in the jailer's face
And start my life with you there next to me

And then I think I know I'll never have
The courage to escape this cage; it's clear
That even if my jailer would allow it
I lack the strength to fly away from here

Each morning here, behind the cage's bars,
A child looks at me, and then smiles at me,
And if I start to sing a cheerful song
He forms his lips into a kiss for me

And if, O sky, I one day want to leave
This silent prison cell and fly away
What shall I say to that child's weeping eyes?
"Forgive me, I'm a captive bird," I'll say

I am a candle, with my burning heart
I fill with light the ruins that surround me;
And if I choose now to be dark and silent
I will undo the household that's around me

★

The Ring

A little girl giggled and said,
"This golden ring, what is its secret?
What's the secret of this ring that grips
My finger so tightly? Take it!

"What's the secret of this shining ring,
This ring that's so bright and glittering?"
The man was puzzled and replied,
"But your good fortune, life itself, is in this ring."

And everyone cried, "Congratulations!"
The little girl said, "I'm sorry that
I ever doubted what it meant."
The years went by. One night

A woman looked down sadly at the shining ring
And saw there all the days when she had hoped
To have her husband's faithful love . . .
Hopes that had come to nothing, nothing at all.

With what bewilderment the woman cried,
"Alas, I see this ring that glitters still,
That shines like this, it is the ring
Of servitude, of slavery."[75]

★

Sin

I sinned, a sin that was all pleasure,
Within the fiery warmth of his embrace
I sinned within his arms
That were like iron, ardent, fierce.

Within that intimately silent darkness
I stared at his mysterious eyes,
My heart convulsive in my trembling breast
As I perceived the longing in his eyes

Within that intimately silent darkness
I sat beside him in a turmoil of uncertainty—
His lips spilled their desire on mine
And I escaped my crazy heart's long misery

I whispered in his ear the words of love,
"I want you, O my love,
I want your arms around me, giving life,
I want you, O my crazy love"

Desire's flame flickered in his eyes
And red wine danced within the glass—
My body in the yielding mattress, drunk
With love, and trembling on his breast

I've sinned, a sin that was all pleasure,
Beside his body, trembling, hardly conscious—
O God, what do I know of what I did
Within that intimately silent darkness?

*

Bathing

To bathe my body in the waters of a spring
I took my clothes off in the mild warm air
Night's silence tempted my sad heart
To tell its sorrows to the waters there

How cool the water was! The glistening ripples
Murmured around me, as if in love with me,
As if with gentle crystal hands they drew
My soul and body into them completely

From far away a wind blew, and in no time
Scattered a flowery chaplet on my hair
Wild pennyroyal's lovely pungent scent
Assailed my nostrils from the breathing air

My eyes closed, I was silent, emptied of emotion
As there against the soft fresh grass my body pressed
Just like a woman nestling in her lover's arms—
I slipped into the water gently and at rest

And suddenly the water's trembling thirsty lips
Were kissing my legs with feverish intensity . . .
I was content to let them, as if happy-drunk—
My flesh, the sinful water's soul, made one in me

★

The Broken Mirror

Yesterday, in memory of you, and of
Our heartfelt love, I thought to wear
My green blouse; I stared at my face in the mirror,
And slowly took the hair-band from my hair

I dabbed my head and breasts with scent,
Round my coquettish eyes I penciled kohl
I shook my hair out over my shoulders,
Slowly, at my mouth's corner, I placed a mole

Then to myself I said, "How sad that he's not here
To be bewitched by my flirtatious guile,
To see my green blouse on my body, and to say
'How lovely you look now,' and smile

"As he's not here to stare at my black pupils
And see the image of his own face there
Why spread my hair like this tonight? Where are
His fingers, to make their home within my hair?

"But he's not here to fall into my arms,
To be made crazy by the perfume of my breast
O mirror, I could die with all this longing and regret
And he's not here to clasp my body to his chest."

I stared at the mirror as it heard me out, and said
"Can you solve this problem of mine? Is there some way?"
It broke, and cried out to express its grief,
"O woman, You've broken my heart, what can I say?"

★

In Love with Sadness

I wish I were like fall . . . I wish I were like fall
I wish I were like fall, silent, with no desires at all
My wishes' leaves would one by one turn sallow-gold
My eyes' sun would grow cold
The heaven of my breast would fill with pain
And suddenly a storm of grief would seize my heart
Like rain my tears would start
And stain my dress
Oh . . . how lovely then, if I were like the fall
Feral and bitter, with colors seeping into one another, so
   beautiful
In my eyes a poet would read . . . a heavenly poem
In my chest a lover's heart would flare with fire
And in its sparks a hidden pain
My song . . .
Like a breeze's voice, with broken wings,
The scent of grief would drip on hearts grown tired of
   things.
In front of me
The bitter face of a new winter:
Behind me
Summer's sudden love, all its commotion.
My breast
The home of sadness, pain, suspicion
I wish I were like fall . . . I wish I were like fall

★

A Wind-Up Doll

More than all this, oh yes,
More than all this one can remain silent
For long hours, one can stare
Motionless, with the fixed gaze of the dead

At a cigarette's smoke
At a cup's shape
At the faded flowers on the rug
At an imaginary line on the wall

With a dry claw
One can pull the curtains aside and see
Rain pelting down in the street
A child with his colored kites

Standing in an archway
A clapped-out old cart hurrying noisily
From the empty square

One can stay where one is
Next to the curtains, but blind, deaf

One can scream
In an utterly absurd voice that's all lies,
"I love . . ."

In a man's strong arms
One can be a beautiful healthy female,
With a body like a leathern cloth
With two large firm breasts

In the bed of a drunkard, a fool, a drifter
One can sully an innocent love

With sly contempt one can make fun
Of every marvelous mystery

One can solve a crossword puzzle alone
One can feel pleased with oneself alone, for finding a
    pointless answer
Yes, a pointless answer, one with five or six letters

One can kneel for a lifetime
With one's head bowed before a cold shrine
One can see God in an unnamed grave
One can find faith in a worthless coin
One can rot in a mosque's cubicles

Like an old reciter of pilgrims' prayers
One can be like zero, always the same
Through subtraction, addition, multiplication . . .
One can think of your eyes, cocooned in their anger,
Like colorless buttons on an old shoe
In the pit of oneself, one can dry up like water

Ashamed, one can hide the beauty of a moment
As if it were a ridiculous black and white snapshot
At the bottom of a chest.

In the frame of an empty day one can place
The picture of someone convicted, defeated, crucified
One can cover the crack in the wall with masks

One can get by with more futile pictures than this
One can be like wind-up dolls

Seeing one's own world with glass eyes
Lying in a baize-lined box
With a body stuffed with straw

Lying for years in folds of spangled tulle
And at every shameless squeeze of one's hand
One can cry out for no reason and say,
"Oh, how happy I am, so happy!"

★

Couple

Night comes
and after night, darkness
after darkness
eyes
hands
and breathing, breathing, breathing
and the sound of water
that falls drip drip drip from the faucet
then two
red dots
from two lit cigarettes
the ticking of the clock
and two hearts
and two lonelinesses

Tahereh Saffarzadeh
1936–2008

Born in Sirjan, in the southeast of Iran, Tahereh Saffarzadeh
was a prolific poet, and having declared that "faith is the only
source of deliverance from the wasteland of contemporary Iran,"
she became a prominent supporter of the Islamic Revolution
of 1979. In addition to her poetry she wrote extensively on
theological subjects, including a book on translations of the
Qor'an, as well as her own bilingual translation of the Qor'an
into Persian and English.[76]

★

Neighbor

> My neighbor
> is a symbol of men in the city
> each morning
> he slowly in his mind
> counts the steps down
> and in the middle of the steps
> he straightens his tie
> blocking the way
>
> My neighbor
> is grave and polite
> in the way that modest traditional brides are
> from beneath his eyelids he watches
> for the luck of a bridegroom
> to appear on some favorable road
> and turn this dull sluggish life
> into something exciting
> into something fortunate

★

Birthplace

I haven't seen my birthplace

the place where my mother
beneath a ceiling
laid down her body's heavy burden
it's still living
the first tick-tock of my little heart
in the stove's chimney
in the crevices between the old bricks;
and the place of that ashamed look
is still visible on the room's door and walls
my mother's look
at my father
and my grandfather

her smothered voice said
"It's a girl"
The midwife trembled
worried about her fee for cutting the cord
knowing there'd be no circumcision celebration

The first time I visit my birthplace
I'll strip my mother's ashamed look
from the wall
and there, where the distinct beating of my pulse began,
I'll make my declaration:
in my unsullied hands
there's no lust to clench my fists or strike out

I'm not going to get roaring drunk
I don't think it's glorious to kill people
I wasn't raised at the table
of male supremacy

★

Walls

Walls are on the move
walls have started to talk
silent submissive walls
walls subservient to the palace
walls bent over by the government
—all from the breath of masses surging forward
ancient walls

      middle-aged
these blind witnesses of tragic events
these silent witnesses of oppression and torture
have now begun to talk
have now begun to move
have now stepped forward
but how quickly they are striding forward
these children
who have now begun to talk
these old men
who are now moving forward[77]

Mina Assadi
Born 1943

Born in Sari, Iran, Mina Assadi has worked as a journalist, and has written songs for a number of well-known Iranian singers, as well as numerous books of poetry. Much of her poetry is on political subjects, and she has been an outspoken opponent of the government of Iran's Islamic Republic. She lives in Stockholm, Sweden.

★

The Dictator's Message

O poets
return,
we have swept
your homeland clean
of thorns and splinters

O writers
return,
to make a record of your works
we have ordered paper from all over the world

O mothers
return,
we have made all the prisons
into schools and universities

O young people
return,
and for your country's future
lay a new foundation

O painters
return,
and on war's blood-soaked walls
paint the white dove of peace

O architects
return,
and for all these returnees
build houses over the corpses
of their dead, who stayed and struggled

*

There's sunshine and the days are dark
there's moonlight and I can't see
there's a veil hanging before my eyes
this season is a season of flight and being silent
a season of being lost in an onslaught of ruin
a season of sleeplessness and distress

this season is a season for cutting down branches
a season of the gallows, of torture and sentencing
a season of cells crowded together
a season for forgetting prison

a season that's good for buying and eating and sleeping
this season is a season of "What's it to me?"
a season of opportunity, of simplified spelling,
a season of profit and loss and assessing the right time
for closing Marx and reading the Qor'an
a season of bragging in poems with fake language
a season of "me, me," of lies and pretension
a season of sucking up to oneself with a microphone
a season of the viruses of fame and reputation
a season of going along with "Death to the Leader"
and then sleeping in a corner of one's house
I'm forgotten and decency is silent
And you are hanging from love's gallows

There's sunshine and the days are dark
there's moonlight and I can't see

Nazanin Nezam Shahidi
1954–2004

Nazanin Nezam Shahidi was born in Tehran and graduated from Tehran University with an MA in Arabic Language and Literature. Her first book of poems was well received, and she was about to publish her second book when she died unexpectedly at the age of fifty.

★

Game

Another moment
we stop
because of a dream

as a solitary child pauses
from her game
when her purple kite
unexpectedly tears
and a gasp of air suddenly
catches in her throat

Another moment
the dream in the sand castle
collapses

castles with no knights
ramparts with no princesses walking there

But for another moment
give me love
so that I can draw a line
on the walls of the world
to my own extent

where it stops
that's where I stop

Fevzieh Rahgozar Barlas

Born 1955

Fevzieh Rahgozar Barlas was born in Balkh, in northern Afghanistan, and graduated from Istanbul University in 1977. She briefly worked for the Afghan Ministry of Information and Culture, and in 1979 she went into exile; she has an MA from the University of Washington (1996).

★

An Innocent Little Girl

The little girl is innocent
they've put henna on her hands
they've plaited her hair beautifully
they've put kohl round her eyes
they've dyed her eyebrows
they've applied red and white makeup to her doll-like face
like poor girls' tattered dolls
she now looks ridiculous

The little girl is innocent
she doesn't see herself
she's dazzled by her blouse that's woven with gold thread
the room smells of old rose-water, milk, and sweat
breath suffocates within their chests
the women sing and dance with tambourines and
    little drums
the little girl smiles

Women tie white flowers for good fortune,
and second-hand gold jewelry
within her ringlets that are wet with sweat

The little girl thinks
                she is a doll
the little girl is innocent
she doesn't know anything

Her mother looks at her
emptily staring, the hollows of her eyes
filled with pain
in his own world, her father
                counts the money
and the old bridegroom
                is really happy

The little girl is innocent
she doesn't know the difference between henna and blood
they've prepared her beautifully
for weeping,
she doesn't know, she doesn't know . . .

Soheila Amirsoleimani

Born 1960

Soheila Amirsoleimani is an Associate Professor of Persian Studies at the University of Utah; her scholarly work is mainly concerned with eleventh-century Persian historical texts. She writes poetry in both Persian and English.

★

Ghazni

This family whose story I am writing[78]
took the name of a city
to the east of Khorasan
this city's name is Ghazni
they came from beyond the River Syr Darya
they came as slaves and became kings
they came powerless and became powerful
and sat among the scribes of Khorasan
among the scribes of Balkh and Nayshapur and Bayhaq
from the court in Bokhara they learned the ceremonies
   of sovereignty[79]
from the court in Bokhara they acquired the custom
   of writing
they were horsemen armed with bows and arrows
they became fine calligraphers, eloquent speakers
and trampled down Indian temples
they plundered the treasures of India
they sat among the scholars of Khwarazm[80]

with Khwarazmi and Biruni[81]
Farrokhi and Onsori and Manuchehri wrote poetry
   for them[82]
Bayhaqi and Maymandi and Ali Qarib sat in their
   courts[83]
This family whose story I am writing
hanged Hasanak[84]
this family whose story I am writing
left Hasanak on the gallows as a spectacle
for seven years
this family became dust, the dust
of their glory can be seen in Lashkar Bazaar

This family whose story I am writing
took the name of a city
a city to the east of Khorasan
the name of this city
is Ghazni

Farzaneh Khojandi
Born 1960

Farzaneh Khojandi was born in Khojand, in northern Tajikistan;
she is considered to be the foremost contemporary Tajik poet.

★

Like an uninhabited island, I'm getting used to silence
Forgotten one, my fame approaches your rare presence

Being alone is a pleasure, a pleasure you'll discover,
And after that you won't want embraces from a lover

Like the sky, I don't want the clothes of hypocrisy
Better a shroud than such a cloak of misery

At thirty-six, like a child, there's weeping in one's heart
It's too late for a season of wild desires to start

A sensitive heart draws someone looking for affection
When could your light shoulders accept such a
   heavy burden?

You told me, "You don't know that tasting apples
   is forbidden"
But in the apple juice the vendors sell that taste is hidden . . .

Beneath the evil skies there are six kinds of feebleness;
Where can one search for Seyavash, for strength true
   men possess?[85]

Azita Ghahreman
Born 1962

Born in Mashhad, Azita Ghahreman has made her home in
Sweden since 2006. As well as books of poetry in Persian, she
has written three books in Swedish.

★

Alleys in a Far-off Land

I still dream
of my red bicycle
on the green shore of summer,
of the shadow of my hair
spread out in the water
and my homework
spattered with grape-seeds.
Getting older,
growing tall, was difficult
in a place of thorns and stones
letting the rainbow-colored marbles slip from my hand,
    one by one
without a playmate
sitting at the side of the alley
with a rusty bicycle in a shed
a photograph of green highways on the wall.

★

Eve

I come from a land of ancient days
from Eve's simple anxieties,
Mariam's gnostic sorrow[86]
Rahil's fourteen years of waiting[87]
Zuleikha's tormented longing[88]
I was always wandering in search of your beautiful face
O love.
I injured myself
and stayed awake all night
chanting your name
and my days were all spent
searching for your voice
as if it could be heard in the breeze.
The thousand years of my life
are a hidden waiting
in the breath of the Judas trees and waves and spring.
All of my moments
are simply a commentary
on the scent of your presence
the shadow of your passing by
and your leaving me

In the desert of longing for what's gone[89]
despised
I am stranded there, in my thirst,
like Hagar

Parween Pazhwak

Born 1967

Parween Pazhwak was born in Kabul, and is from a prominent literary and diplomatic family. She completed a medical degree, intending to practice in Afghanistan, but became a refugee after the Soviet invasion of Afghanistan in 1979 and sought asylum in Canada.

★

Mother's Shared Blouse

I put your blouse on, mother
and the scent of our house
the scent of smiles and kindness and trust
the scent of our garden
with the caged canaries' twittering
the scent of the window
with our neighbor's rooster crowing
the scent of bread
the scent of people's sorrow
the scent of the flowers our father planted in our garden
the scent of the angry wind blowing from the martyrs'
    graves overwhelmed me

I put your blouse on, mother
and the sound of the pigeons in our house's passageway
    filled my heart with their cooing

I put your blouse on, mother
and went back to you
to your kind world
to my own familiar earth
to beloved Kabul!

I put your blouse on, mother
and found my sisters again
and found my friends again
and my hopes came back to me one by one
and I saw once again
the reflection of my smile in the brail
of green water in our water-tank

I put your blouse on, mother
and I called on God
with the name I called Him when I was a child
and I prayed for you, mother
I prayed for you . . .

If I wrap your blouse
around our wild almond tree
it will blossom

If I spread it over
the dried-up twigs of our grape-vine
it will cast shade

If I entrust your blouse
to the wind
once again lights will shine in the foothills of
   our mountains,
Aseh and Shirdarvazeh

If I let your blouse
wander in the alleyways
the orphans will find clothes

If I could divide up
your blouse, they would not be able
to divide up our land!

If the dried-up well in our garden
could remember your blouse
it would give water again
it would give to our hearts
an image of morning and sunlight
and we would all remember
the shared blouse of our mother
the shared blouse of our mother . . .

Khaledeh Forugh

Born 1972

A native of Kabul, Khaledeh Forugh has an MA in Persian Language and Literature from Kabul University and a PhD from the National University of Tajikistan in Doshanbeh. She is a member of the Department of Persian Studies at Kabul University, and has published numerous books of poetry, a novel, and a volume of literary criticism.

★

It Came from the Past

It came here from the past, it came in its magnificence,
Rudaki was its presence, and Rabe'eh its innocence[90]
Its green eyes glittered with the vividness of life itself,
Life's waters flowed within its poets' lyrics and laments.
It came here from the past, through complicated branching
   ways,
It opened roads from roads, they were its guide and
   its defense,
It came here from the past as if it sang like Nakisa,[91]
From King Parviz's time it brought its regal radiance,[92]
And in its voice was music sorrow gave and Barbad played,[93]
His song a river, and his voice a moon of eloquence.
Its breaths were Avicenna's and its steps were Ferdowsi's,
And it was blasphemy and faith and known experience;
The steps of Ferdowsi paced out a noble epic meter[94]
And Avicenna's breaths sought knowledge and intelligence—[95]

Knowledge was his intent, and his beginning too
    was knowledge,
A spirit from the past accompanied his search for sense,
It came out of the past and it was nourished by the past
And from the past it brought the day of his accomplishments.
The palace of the first Darius was its royal home
And his Atossa's eyes, Atossa's eyes, its residence;[96]
It gave its stature to the towering castle of Jamshid
And with its cloak it hid the ladder of his arrogance.[97]
It came here from the past and it was agony or fire—
Hafez was all its tears, and they were its deliverance,[98]
And it was poetry or pain, a history or tradition,
Its veins were Bayhaqi, the *Masnavi* its glorious sense.[99]
It trod the alleys of existence in its modern form
And from the past a reed flute's tones were its accompaniments.
It raised love's hand, and gradually it grew and it matured,
Its prayer was Mowlavi's for all that freedom represents—
It was the most lost fantasy and the most endless bridge
And Shams's burning love, and all his unrestrained laments;[100]
It came here from the past and was it strong now or grown
    weak?
Whence did it come, and where was it, that knew no hence
    or whence?
It came here from the past, the ancestor of all the world,
And saw that it was blessed now by its own essential sense.

★

208   *The Mirror of My Heart*

These ancient mountain slopes are poets, even so,
Escaped now from themselves, contemporaries
  we know,
These ancient mountain slopes, the winds' assault
  by night,
They've traveled here from many, many years ago.
Home to the sleepers in the cave they're full of life[101]
Within the empty alleys of the world they wander to
  and fro
And they were there, confronting Moses' heart,
As they were passers-by of weeping Farhad's woe.[102]
They nourish myths, their poems are ambiguous,
They're visible, high summits thrust up from below;
They've burned within themselves, they're lost
  within themselves
Though lost beyond all loss they're near at hand,
  and though
Their voices seethe with silence, still
The last word's always theirs, both now and long ago;
They are the high imaginings of God
These ancient mountain slopes are poets, even so.

Mandana Zandian
Born 1972

Born in Esfahan, Dr. Mandana Zandian is a graduate of Shahid
Beheshti Medical School in Tehran, and is currently a research
oncologist at Cedars-Sinai Hospital in Los Angeles. She moderates
a weekly Persian-language radio program on poetry and related
cultural subjects.

★

Death too will grow old one day
he'll become weary
and sit down,
he'll bend over, with his head on his knees
he'll hug himself, like life
and stretch out his hands, hesitantly, in the alphabet of
   stone fragments, walls, and
drag words out of the dark earth's depths and
bring them together, sculpt them, break off bits
in a faded voice
and he'll think the moon
is a kinder glance for leaving, and
love
a past more complete than the road, and
he'll stand up
draw breath, blink
freed
on the threshold of the short pause
that is life

★

Words are alive
they breathe
they dream
they make love and
like pain
they twist in death's waist
they give up the ghost and
they become poems and
they remain . . .
we are not alone;
we are wandering birds
that do not wake up
from words' dream

Mana Aqai
Born 1973

Mana Aqai was born in Bushehr, on the Persian Gulf, and moved
to Sweden with her family in 1978. She has an MA in Iranian
Languages from Uppsala University, and now lives in Stockholm,
where she works as a professional translator.

*

You said: "Be the bride of my dreams
and I'll come and wake you with seven kisses"
and seven times you wrote "black" to break the red spell
and seven times I went under the snow
so that one by one snowflakes would rest on my eyelids
and the velvet of my dreams would grow more white
and this is how seven nights and seven days passed for me
from the moment that the story's wicked stepmothers
saw themselves as more beautiful in the mirror
every night I say, The prince is on his way, he'll arrive
every night seven young horses neigh in my dreams
and I start up seven times
and I see seven men behind the window-panes
all dwarfs

*

Stains

They came late
out of narrow suffocating passageways
like bloodstains
from cuts on the fingers of a sleepless woman
they spilled onto the paper
and couldn't be washed out
or cleaned with a handkerchief

behind each one
there was an unhealed scar
an unspoken pain
and a cry that, out of fear,
was imprisoned in cells' depths

they were uneven red circles
my poems
and the more I looked at them
they grew wider and wider
until one day my eyes
couldn't see the white spaces anymore

Pegah Ahmadi

Born 1974

Pegah Ahmadi was born in Tehran and studied Persian Literature at the University of Tehran. She published three books of poetry in Iran, which were subsequently banned due to her political outspokenness. Ahmadi left the country as a political refugee in 2009, and has since lived in the West. She has published ten books in all, two of which have been translated into German; she has also translated a volume of Sylvia Plath's poetry into Persian.

★

Why in the depths of no-progress is nothing moving?
language is a cutting off of terror
look, blood doesn't flow from the wrist,
and neither does it clot
and I, whose eye was an open history of intensity,
throw a razor into the abyss.
Drag me into the street
that is the dark castle of life
look back at your shadow, so that it won't fall from the rope.
Nothing is more frightening than when nothing happens
how does language die?
where does it make an absence?
cut me off, so that my being will gush out
take me as a whole
and cut me into pieces
the revolution has collapsed
and for half a century love has been a monster.

Stand here, on the harp,
and bring something
to consciousness in me
bring me the symphony's invoices
a shattered forehead
in which a spear is hidden
and the neck choked by amber
Oh, you locked jowl!
Am I language, that I bind you up with a fissure
spin my body round
are you language? To blow me up?
Why in the depths of no progress is nothing moving?
Give a signature to my bruised neck
ascend a vein
and make a leaden face
that will shine on the ceiling;
with a half-drunk tongue of intensity
it cannot sleep
the revolution has collapsed
and for half a century love has been a monster

Granaz Moussavi
Born 1976

Granaz Moussavi was born in Tehran; in 1997 she and her family emigrated to Australia. She has a postgraduate degree in film editing from Flinders University, Australia. Moussavi's poetry has been widely translated into a number of languages; she is also a film-maker and has made a number of well-received films, including *My Tehran for Sale* (2008) and *1001 Nights* (2006), a documentary on Iranian poets in exile.

★

The Blue Headscarf's Words

> I could be wearing all the clouds in the world
> and they'd still throw a cloak over my shoulders
> so that I wouldn't be naked
> here the moon shines in the dusk
> the hand that hits me
> doesn't know
> that sometimes a minnow
> can fall in love with a whale
> there's no point in their shouting at me
> they don't know
> that I've become a fish now
> that your river's gone over my head
> I don't want to wear the world's deserts
> or to breathe
> on a planet that hasn't yet been discovered

even if they take the wind's fingerprints
they won't discover the trace of your kiss

We must go into the street
although the cars pass between us and the sun
we must go into the street
all this sky won't fit into the window

I want to sunbathe
in the southernmost part of your soul
the ceiling light isn't worth the pains of hell
the one who draws the curtains
            doesn't know
always the sound of the person standing on the other
   side of the line
            tomorrow he'll arrive
whatever they want, it's all right
            they'll tear off the door's hinges
tonight I'll come from the dusky moonlight
and I'll cut into pieces all the curtains and cloaks
and leave them to make kites, and for moonlit nights
they'll rent a room in the world's suburbs
and I shall have gone
I want to give my blouse to the sun

★

Strike! Seventy lashes
so that I'll become more of a woman
beside the stones
and my body will fill with pomegranates[103]

I won't repent
"Stand aside! Halt!"
they've been through my pockets
and there's no other thought there
than the sun, that is sick of veils

Sara Mohammadi-Ardehali

Born 1976

Sara Mohammadi-Ardehali was born and currently lives in Tehran, and has an MA degree in Sociology from Tehran's Alameh Tabatabai University.

★

A Full-Time Position

> No man wants
> to fall in love with a woman
> who works in a circus
>
> one of those women who has to walk a tight-rope
>
> He falls in love with a woman
> who might fall at any moment
>
> and if she doesn't fall
> thousands of people clap their hands
> to applaud her

★

Woman

Everything is obvious
at thirty-five
without
your having to be naked

★

The Smell of Blood

I swim
from this side to that
I go underwater
for as long as I can hold my breath
I trail my fingers along the bottom of the pool
suddenly
the memory of you
returns, swimming toward me like a shark

★

Difficult Evening

My hand
stretches toward the telephone
it comes back again

like a child to whom they've said
the cakes on the table
are for guests

★

Meeting

Like a leopard
he emerged
from among the bushes
with Genghis Khan's smile on his lips
his black eyes flickered
he held out his hand

the poets of Nayshapur
the multi-colored silks of Balkh
the granaries of Khorasan and Khwarazm[104]
in me
went up in flames
and turned to smoke

I shook his hand

*

Empire of Dust

I forgot
my body's handwriting
my shoulders' calligraphy and the contour of my laughter
I must be naked
I'll go beneath the sun
beside the wind

I went on a trip
the Mediterranean laughed at me

it said
Why are you afraid of the water?
The Persian empire has fallen
we've agreed on summer
come, with old Phoenician mariners
we'll go sailing

*

A complete mess

Wearing comfortable slippers
he gets going
he picks up the half-open books under the bed
he folds the scattered clothes
he collects the pencils and cups
he comes behind your head
he hesitates
then brings his lips close to the softness of your ear
you sense the sound of his breath

you turn round

the room is empty
it's a complete mess

*

Confession

I had a relationship with him
I was alone
and he was alone too
we were both tired
I of the earth
he of the sky
our rendezvous was at midnight
he came to the window
you won't believe it
he smiled at me
he was very beautiful
extraordinarily beautiful

I remember
it was the fourteenth night
and
he
was complete, full

Shabnam Azar

Born 1977

Shabnam Azar's work as a journalist led to her having to leave Iran in 2009. She has a postgraduate degree in media arts from the Academy of Media Arts in Cologne, and has published four books of poetry in Iran and Germany.

★

Stop

> Emptier than an abandoned house
> emptier than the leftovers of a splendid party
> emptier than a door left half open
> a hand that has reached for something
> and is left in the air, waiting
> a rotted flag
> faded and worn
> old
>
> I look at the days that have gone
> at the faded colors of old photographs
> at a mouth
> that has not yet forgotten how to laugh
>
> no matter how strong
> the pillar
> the house finally collapses
> sounds
> finally end in silence
> and shadows
> return into things

tomorrow
breathes
greedily
and this old clock
whose white face is hung in the room's cold air,
for all its life
thinks of the silence between tick and tock

★

Free Fall

Alone

he ran on

a few steps ahead of me
before he fell
on the road to freedom

freedom is beautiful

even
when you're in free fall
toward death
even
when you grow cold
lying in your own blood

Bullets!
dear bullets
please
go back to your shell casings
and we too
will go back to our homes

Rosa Jamali
Born 1977

Born in Tabriz, Rosa Jamali has an MA in English Literature
from Tehran University. As well as poetry, she has written a play,
Shadows (2007), and has translated W. B. Yeats into Persian.

*

A shortcut to an unknown spot (a crime that I've revealed)

With your permission
We'll assess whether this unknown sign is correct
the crime that I've revealed
they've exiled me to an unknown spot
and it's no distance from being underground

Speak, say something, confess!
I came into the world on the day you stroked my shroud
my constant entertainment was a dark loophole
my evidence a page from my sister's identity card
they ascertain the strength of gravity the moment a stone
doesn't sink in water
Speak, say something, confess!
the crime that I've revealed

The crime that I've revealed

That's great!
I don't know if it's four o'clock or five
if today's Thursday or Friday

if it's October or November
if it's winter or autumn
minutes are halted, forbidden
I'm guilty of murdering someone
it's not the first time
it's not the last time
it's the thousandth time they've put me in prison
I have thirty seconds
for years my shadow has followed your shadow
my hair is a tangled spider's web
there's algae between my fingers
I won't look into your pupils anymore
you've spilled cold milk on my bones
you've shot a volley of bullets into my pupils
for thirty-five days I've been in love with corpses
though this is an inaccurate account
That's great!
his eyeballs are cloudy with pneumonia
my breasts feel crushed
they give me a blind man's stick
and looking at the calendar is forbidden
That's great!
A woman is screaming, vertical and horizontal, at eighty
  degrees on the clock from the welts the stick makes
        a woman is screaming round the clock
        a woman is screaming, a few seconds, a
           moment of surrender, it's ninety degrees
        a woman is screaming and the gashes and a
           wall-clock, one hundred and eighty degrees
        a woman is screaming / it's half past midnight /
           the circle's complete
        it's three hundred and sixty degrees

A revolver's diagonal shape on the wall
the smell of blood's sent me crazy
Speak, say something, confess!
it looks like bad weather's coming
the world is a short woman who's been slashed down
Speak, say something, confess!
they've exiled me to an unknown spot
a slab of rubble drops into water
and it's no distance from being underground

    a woman is screaming . . .
    a woman is screaming . . .
    a woman is screaming . . .

Hengameh Hoveyda
Born 1978

Born in Tehran, Hengameh Hoveyda has a bachelor's degree in Persian Literature; she currently lives in Paris, where she is pursuing a doctorate at the Sorbonne.

Loneliness

> Fold yourself in your embrace
> embrace yourself and sleep
> this is the only thing you have
> your hands
>
> if you don't put your trust in loneliness
> like a scarecrow swaying back and forth in the wind
> your hands
> will become a nest for crows
> and they've stolen your eyes . . .

The Criminal

> They have exiled me in myself
> so far away
> that neither my voice reaches anyone else
> nor anyone else's reaches me

Fatemeh Shams
Born 1983

Born in Mashhad, Fatemeh Shams left Iran in 2006 and settled in England. She studied first at the Agha Khan University in London, and then at Oxford, where she was awarded a PhD in Iranian Studies. She has published two collections of poetry in Persian, and a selection of her poems has been translated into English. In 2012 she received the Zhaleh Esfahani poetry award in London for the best young Iranian poet. She is currently Assistant Professor of Modern Persian Literature at the University of Pennsylvania.

★

Never to fall asleep . . .

Never to fall asleep, because of a nightmare's fear
To sit awake each night until the dawn is here
Caught between waking and sleep, as if unsteady with drink,
In the name of life to die, with blindness drawing near

In futile empty love repeated endlessly
In saying, "I love you, my dear! Do you love me?"
In wanting things that reach their end but never start,
In pointless work, in no work's sour banality

To have no memory, no border, and no place,
To drift about in men's and women's cold embrace,
To drag with you a suitcase and three hundred books
To have, among all colors, a shroud's conceal your face

To tear my heart from those who wore a mask and all
    they mean
From men whose inward being is a reeking foul latrine
To tear my heart from that strange city of my childhoods
Whose earth holds sorrow still that's innocent and clean

From endless hesitating, from not returning there,
In waking dreams without you, in exile's arms and air,
In boundless longing for the things I'll never see
In "hope," that lovely word whose absence brings despair

Without a homeland, without love, in wild perplexity,
Within this narrow cul-de-sac from which I can't walk free
To vomit you from me, and ah to ask you with my love
"O wounded, worn-out country! Do you still think of me?"

★

W for War (3)

In memory of Aziz and the children of war in Kobane[105]

How hard it was to stay alive
In the war, the bullets' rain,
When everywhere they looked
Were death and darkness and pain

They had to pack and leave
And travel to who-knows-where
To a geography unknown,
That was anywhere but there

Behind them their lost home
Was black with ash, ahead
A hard uneven road
And the flood of those who fled

His shoulders carried a child
His arms were around another,
Behind them ran a third
Like a mound that dust-clouds smother

Their mother was following them
A mountain of silence and dread,
Eye to eye with the war, tears flowed
Like pomegranate juice, blood-red.

Ah, but the war was brutal
Destroying her hopes with fear,
Stealing her children's joy
With its thuggish, violent sneer.

Three children—one didn't smile,
Three children—one had a fever,
They were homeless and silent now
Like a poem unheard forever

By the side of the road, bewildered
By the kindness of the sun,
Perhaps someone would come
And see him there, someone . . .

War came in the shape of a man,
Death came in the form of the sun
His eyes were fixed on the sky, frozen
Forever, and seeing no one

And then he saw nothing forever,
And forever now he kept
His silence, and closed his infant eyes
On the crimes around him, and slept.

★

Prosecution

Pictures don't lie
I've grown old
and I've forgotten the love I felt when I was twenty
you've come too late
paper's grown expensive
postmen have had enough
planes mostly crash
and no one else's file will ever be closed

★

Roots

Once I was a tree
with black and white crows in my hair
with upside-down roots
the ground had set my body free,
my body, my roots,
roots that were the crows' refuge
once I was everything
a dream filled with life in a year of famine.

Fatemeh Ekhtesari
Born 1986

Fatemeh Ekhtesari was born in the town of Kashmar in the northeast of Iran. As a young women she trained as a midwife, but after enrolling at the University of Tehran she turned her attention to literature. Virtually from the beginning her writing attracted censorship and state condemnation. Her status as a poetic gadfly was confirmed when she took part in a poetry festival in Gothenburg, Sweden, in 2013; on her return to Iran, she was arrested and tried for immoral behavior and blasphemy and was sentenced to ninety-nine lashes and eleven years' imprisonment. She left Iran illegally and made her way to Scandinavia, where she now lives.

★

I was knocked up and made pregnant
By a right-wing political bore
When the dust had settled he'd left me
As if I were a whore

An artist signed my belly
He was a real celebrity
He took a selfie with my tears,
Planted a kiss on my misery

The lefties shouted, "Abort it!"
Their hammer and sickle attacked me,
The placards in their bloody hands
Were claiming that they backed me

The feminists gave me an essay[106]
About what some big-shot has done
Spit on his sex-obsessed mind
Not a mind but a pond full of scum

"Hey bitch, the world's in an uproar . . ."
My mom declares, "Your life's ok,
Call her 'Nazanin Zahra,'
But you're a disgrace—Enough's enough, I say!"

I'm a painting, a ditch,
The woman in each picture, more or less,
Like a spot of blood in the toilet
Like Iran on the map, colorless.

★

Gently I'll take them off
All the things on my body, my clothes,
A few arsenals of arms, gunpowder,
There's a battlefield under my blouse

Naked, like the first time
Naked, like a knife that's bleeding
Naked, in front of your eyes
Like the forbidden poem you're reading

Gently I'll take them out
The books in each bookcase
The killed heroes will rise in my soul
Triumphantly in place

Hafez's and Eliot's infamous eyes[107]
Weary Samsa's hardened claws[108]
Sex with Don Quixote, Ali Baba,
And rape as a matter of course

My skin's a book cover that's torn,
A book of woes, I'm scarcely alive,
Our whole world's an underground
Like *Slaughterhouse-Five*[109]

My joy is nothing but footnotes,
My happiness mislaid in sorrow
365 *Nights of Sodom*[110]
365 days of torture

Come on, pour paraffin in my mouth
Come on, set fire to the library—
Blow up all my sulks and moods
And vent your fatigue on my body.

★

Cerebral feudalism
My head exploded on the floor, at your feet
You stepped over my head, not noticing, discreet

Surrealism
My eye exploded, in the depths of my glance there's a
    woman
Her pupil is in mid-dream, what's it staring at?

Futurism
My belly exploded, disgusted with the wind in its gut
The pain grew greater; tea please, and make it sweet

Sado-masochistic eroticism
My sex exploded on the table
You enjoyed the blood, every bit was a treat

Religious romanticism
My heart exploded, and my religion's loving you
My tribute is kisses, and hugs when we meet[111]

AgathaChristieism
I exploded from something lost like a loaded rifle
The shadow of a man, in a yard, waiting on a seat

Postmodernism
I exploded from my poems, there were letters—
T . . . A . . . D . . . H . . . N . . . Q . . . P . . . R . . . all
    over the street

Notes

EPIGRAPHS

1. Abbas Amanat, *Iran: A Modern History* (New Haven: 2017), p. 21.
2. *Divan-e Alam Taj Qa'em-Maghami, Zhaleh*, ed. Ahmad Karami (Tehran: 1374/1995), p. 149.

THE MEDIEVAL PERIOD

1. For commentary on this poem, see the Introduction, pp. xv–xxi.
2. Ganjeh is a city in what is now independent Azerbaijan. Because of this poem and others like it, Mahsati is believed to have come from Ganjeh and to have had an affair with the son of a local cleric.
3. The phrase "wine . . . from my eyes" indicates bloody tears that are the color of red wine; the comparison of a heart in love to meat roasting, or grilling over a flame, is commonplace in medieval Persian poetry, and hence in

Asian poetry generally. In Joseph Conrad's *An Outcast of the Islands* (1896), the character Babalatchi contemptuously refers to a Dutchman who has fallen in love with a beautiful Indonesian woman by saying, "She has made roast meat of his heart."

4. This poem is said to have been extemporized by Mahsati when King Sanjar was held up by a fall of snow (the "silver carpet" in line 4). The story goes that Sanjar was so impressed by this impromptu poem that he gave Mahsati a position at his court.

5. The Virgin Mary is revered in Islam; the nineteenth chapter of the Qor'an is devoted to her praise.

6. The last line of the poem means both "I see him in my mind's eye" and "I weep" (at the memory of his loveliness).

7. This poem is an ambiguous riddle. The primary meaning describes the rose of the opening line. In this interpretation the youngster's shirt is the rose petals as they open, "tearing" the bud; the sweat is dew; crimson is the rose's color compared to a blush; the golden coins in the rose's "mouth" are the yellow pollen on the stamens of the rose. But the poem also has an implied bawdy meaning: the "rose that's celebrated everywhere" is a young person famous for his or her beauty, and Persian poets (for example, Hafez) quite often mention a youngster's torn shirt as being erotically attractive (presumably because skin can be glimpsed through the tear); the third line could obviously refer to furtive love-making; the golden coins in this interpretation could be payment for sex, or a bribe to the youngster to keep quiet about the liaison. The last line also explicitly refers to the way that exceptionally fine poems were traditionally rewarded, by the poet's mouth being filled with coins, and so it is a hint to the listener that the poet would welcome payment for her work.

8. The Iranian scholar Eslami Nodushan's note on this poem reads as follows: "The speaker is a female musician-for-hire; the poem indicates the wretched circumstances of such women who did not know what awaited them each day. She has been brought from home and is passed from customer to customer. Whoever gave the more money became her temporary master and could do whatever he wished with her." Mohammad Ali Eslami Nodushan, *Nar daneh-ha* ("Pomegranate Seeds"), (Tehran: 1381/2002), p. 64. Nodushan's note indicates that the profession of musician could easily slide into that of prostitution, and to this day some traditional Iranian families still consider musicians to be disreputable (much in the way that "respectable" families in Victorian England would be horrified by one of their daughters becoming an actress, as this was said to lead to the same fate).

9. The fact that her tears run into her ears, which seems at first to be counter-intuitive, implies that she is lying awake weeping as she thinks about the poem's addressee. The American poet Louise Bogan (1897–1970) uses the same image in one of her poems ("Solitary Observation Brought Back from a Sojourn in Hell"), with the same implication. Louise Bogan, *The Blue Estuaries* (New York: 1968), p. 98.

10. This poem exists in various versions and with varying numbers of lines. The translation includes only the lines that are usually accepted as genuine. The reference to the poet's veil is interesting as it contradicts what a number of contemporary reports indicate, which is that the women of the Mongol nobility often went unveiled; clearly this was not true of all of them. It draws on a Middle Eastern tradition of the veil as a symbol of power or royal authority as much as a symbol of chastity/sexual modesty; the tradition of kings addressing their subjects

from behind a curtain (i.e., "veiled") goes back to the pre-Islamic Sasanian dynasty (224 CE–651 CE). This "royal" meaning of the veil is often invoked in pre-modern Persian poetry, perhaps even more than as an emblem of "chastity" (and poets often seem to conflate the two meanings, as in this poem).

11. It's possible that this poem refers to a metaphorical "exile" (absence) from a lover, but it seems more likely that it is meant literally and was written in the brief period between Padshah Khatun's fall from power, engineered by her enemies at court, and her death.

12. This almost certainly refers to Jahan Khatun's imprisonment after her family was deposed by the warlord Mobarez al-Din.

13. The comparison of the feelings of someone in love to meat in the process of being cooked is quite common in Persian poetry (see note 3). It's especially apt here because the liver was seen as the seat of the affections and animal vitality (so that "I'd grill his liver" means "I'd drive him crazy with desire"). And grilled liver is still a tasty feature of outdoor meals in Iran (it is, for example, a common street food).

14. This poem gives us an image of Jahan Khatun after she had been captured during Mobarez al-Din's conquest of Shiraz. Even though it is meant metaphorically as much as literally, the detail of the "ruined school" is startlingly specific for poetry of this period.

15. Almost certainly a reference to the poet's uncle who was deposed and killed by the warlord Mobarez al-Din in 1353. Usually a cypress in Persian lyric poetry represents a beautiful young person (of either sex), but in this case the image seems to draw on the Near Eastern history of

a "cypress" indicating a sacred tree or a powerful ruler (as in Ezekiel 31—see Nancy Bowen, *Abingdon Old Testament Commentaries: Ezekiel* [Nashville: 2010], p. 192), rather than on the cypress as an image of youthful beauty (as in Theocritus, and *passim* in medieval Persian poetry: see Theocritus 18, the *Epithalamium for Helen,* trans. Robert Wells [Manchester: 1988], p. 114: "So Helen shines . . . a cypress tree that rears / Its dark adornment over field and garden . . ."). I am grateful to an anonymous member of the audience at a talk given at the University of Chicago in October 2018 for pointing this out to me.

16. The cypress here is envisioned as a sacred tree/presence representing God. See the previous note for the possible meanings of "cypress" in Persian poetry.

17. A pun on Jahan Khatun's name (one she often makes): "Jahan" means "world," so "world's lord" means "Jahan's lord," which indicates that she is equating the "friend" she is reproaching with God.

18. "Tartary" is central Asia, from which the most valuable musk came.

19. The story of Jacob's mourning for his son Joseph, when he thinks Joseph is dead although he has in fact been sold into slavery by his brothers, is recounted in both the Hebrew Bible and the Qor'an. Jacob's grief is a common trope in medieval Persian verse, particularly—though not exclusively—in elegies.

20. The sense of the last two lines is: "What happens is not a result of time's vicissitudes but has been fated from eternity."

21. The "new rose" is the poet's daughter.

22. Rezvan is the guardian of the Islamic paradise.

23. David and his psalms: The Psalms of the biblical King David are mentioned by name twice in the Qor'an (4:163 and 17:55), and both he and his psalms are often referred to in Persian poetry.

24. The paradox is deliberate: "Unchanging Fate (i.e., what has been ordained since the beginning of time) ensures that our lives will change."

25. Half-rhymes are so rare in pre-modern Persian poetry as to be virtually unknown, but this poem ends on a half-rhyme in Persian, as in the English translation.

26. The "wretched hovel" is a reference to the world.

27. This is the last poem in Jahan Khatun's *divan* (collected short poems), and it reads as a farewell to life. As poems are arranged in a divan alphabetically according to the rhyme, this means that she has written the poem that signals her farewell to life by using as her rhyme the last letter of the Persian alphabet, so that a poem about the end of her life ends her book.

28. See note 30 below.

29. The sense of the poem is that the "friend" wasn't really interested in her in the first place.

30. The "languid limb" is a euphemism and the line as a whole means "he's impotent." Similar euphemistic phrases, with the same meaning, appear in poems by other poets.

31. "Arezu" is a pun since it is the name of the poem's addressee and it means "longing." Arezu is an exclusively female name, and the poem perhaps indicates a same-sex relationship, or at least the desire for one.

32. The cypress tree is a common metaphor for a beautiful young person, of either sex (see note 15 on p. 242).

FROM 1500 TO THE 1800s

1. The curve of the eyebrows is implicitly compared to the curve at the top of a mehrab, the niche in a mosque that indicates the direction of Mecca, and toward which Moslems bow in prayer. The poet is saying that she bows down to her lover rather than to God, and this is why her prayers "cannot be heartfelt" (line 4). The phrase can also be interpreted in mystical terms, in which case it means that the speaker's allegiance is to Sufism rather than to orthodox Islamic practice.

2. Loqman is a wise sage referred to in chapter 31 of the Qor'an.

3. The poem mixes various motifs (the world is faithless, drink wine to forget your sorrows, orthodox religion is to be rejected in favor of either an earthly or mystical love, no wisdom can circumvent the inevitability of death) that are common in a great deal of Persian lyric verse.

4. The poem is ambiguous; it can mean "I am upset that our friendship is over" or "I was a fool to be friends with you (and trust you) in the first place" or both.

5. Part of the point of this poem lies in the fact that according to Islamic law a man can have more than one wife, but a woman cannot have more than one husband, and so the poet is apparently usurping the male role when she starts out by saying that she'll have two husbands. But then she says that one of the new husbands is for "you" (her present husband), indicating that she will after all be sticking to the

one husband prescribed for her by Islamic law. The fact that she wants to divorce her present husband and hand him over to the "burly Turkoman" implies that she thinks of him as gay, and passively so, which coming from a wife was certainly meant as an insult.

6. Many of the poems translated for this book exist in more than one version, and usually the discrepancies make little difference to the overall meaning. However, the first line of this poem exists in another version that wholly changes what is being said. Here is the alternative version:

> Your chastity's become the cause of my disgrace—
> If you were mad enough that this were not the case
> You would be guilty of an even worse disgrace

7. A rare instance of a poem in Persian that makes fun of the clichés of Persian lyric love poetry. In this way it's a little like Shakespeare's Sonnet 130 ("My mistress' eyes are nothing like the sun . . .").

8. This poem is inscribed on Nur Jahan's tomb in Lahore. She calls herself a "stranger" because after the death of her husband, Jahangir, she was gently but firmly pushed aside. Lamps and roses might well be found in and near the tended mausoleum of someone remembered with affection; but as well as their literal meaning, lamps and roses are common metaphors for the beloved in Persian lyric poetry—lamps being loved by moths (because they cannot resist the lamps' light, in which they are burned), roses by nightingales. The fact that there are no lamps or roses nearby, and that no moths or nightingales come to her tomb, means that she considers herself unloved and forgotten.

9. The ka'bah is the black stone that marks the geographical center of the Islamic world, and around which pilgrims

perambulate. In Islamic tradition it was inaugurated by Ibrahim (Abraham).

10. There are two versions of this line (the difference is a single letter, though this completely changes the sense). The other version can be translated as: "This thing is what you came from, sir."

11. Layli and Majnun are the archetypal separated lovers of Islamic cultures. The story is originally Arabic, but its best known version is the one by Nezami (twelfth century), in Persian. Layli stays at home and does what she is told to do by her family; Majnun wanders in the wilderness and goes mad (his name means "maddened"). The "chain" in the last line refers obliquely to the fact that lunatics were often chained up; Makhfi is saying that although she is not the one sent mad by love, she is as chained up (by shame) as a madman is. The name Layli is Arabic, in which it is pronounced "Layla"; however it is clear that it was pronounced "Layli" in medieval Persian because poets often rhyme on it, and always with the "i" (like "ee" in English) sound.

12. Musk, in the form in which it was used as a scent, is black. A small black mole on a face was considered especially attractive (as was a beauty spot, imitating such a mole, in eighteenth-century Europe).

13. A reference to two irreconcilables, like oil and water, or chalk and cheese, in English, with the added implication that stone can break glass. The "friend" here almost certainly means "God."

14. A reference to Makhfi's real name, "Zib al-Nissa," meaning "Loveliest of Women."

15. Zinat wrote this poem as an inscription for her tomb, which was destroyed in the aftermath of the Indian

Rebellion of 1857 (formerly known as the Indian Mutiny), when the British turned the mosque in which her tomb was located into a bakery. The mosque has now been restored to its original function, but no sign of Zinat al-Nissa's tomb has been found.

16. This poem is said to have made Aysheh famous when, as a teenager, she recited it extemporaneously at the court of Timur Shah Durrani.

17. The poem uses the tropes of erotic verse (the wounded heart, a garden, vowing to be the beloved's slave) with a mystical implication; "My Love" clearly refers to God, and the garden the poet dreams of is paradise.

18. A lament by Aysheh for her son Faiz Talab, who was killed fighting for the Afghan king Timur Shah Durrani during his war for the control of Kashmir. The "you" of the first line is addressed to Faiz Talab himself (reproaches to a child for dying before the speaker are not uncommon in Persian poetry, the most famous example occurring in Ferdowsi's *Shahnameh*, when Ferdowsi unexpectedly breaks off his narrative and inserts a lament for the death of his son), but it could also be taken as referring to God.

19. Farhad is a legendary figure who appears in the romance *Khosrow and Shirin* by Nezami (1141–1209); he is a stone mason who is in love with the princess Shirin and when he hears that Shirin has died (which is untrue), he commits suicide. The fact that Farhad is a figure in a romance leads to the next lines in which a garden and a nightingale are evoked, as they are traditional features of romance poetry and of love poetry in general.

20. At the end of the poem Maluli refers to herself as "Malul" rather than "Maluli"; this shortening of a name (to fit a poem's meter) is not uncommon in pre-modern Persian

poetry (for example, Hafez shortens the name Abu Es'haq to Bu Es'haq in one ghazal).

21. It's interesting that three of Maluli's poems given here imply that she is in love with someone she shouldn't be in love with, perhaps an adherent of another religion. Though this is a common motif in Persian poetry, it's possible that her insistence on this theme had an autobiographical origin.

22. Dervishes were mendicant Sufis, and Sufi writings often implied, or stated quite openly, that all faiths are valid if the believer's heart is sincere.

23. Non-Moslems wore a specific kind of belt to indicate their separate status.

24. Patterns on a hand were usually made by henna (used by both men and women), which looks quite like dried blood; here Mastureh is saying it doesn't just look like blood, it is blood (hers).

25. This poem about Mastureh's husband's absence makes a pair with the following poem ("The candle-brightness of your face . . .") about his arrival home.

26. Khosrow is both the name of the poet's husband and of a legendary pre-Islamic king. This leads the poet to compare herself to another pre-Islamic king, Jamshid, whose pleasure at his own success was so great that he thought himself equal to God.

27. Qebleh is the direction in which the ka'bah in Mecca lies. The notion of the beloved as the poet's own personal qebleh—that is, as the "direction" of her devotion—is common in pre-modern Persian love poetry. Its somewhat blasphemous implication is a part of the effect, as one of

the poetic conventions concerning erotic love is that it makes one forget one's religious obligations.

28. Layli and Majnun are the archetypal "Romeo and Juliet" lovers of Islamic poetry. In common with a number of other women poets who wrote in Persian, Mastureh compares herself to the male of the couple (Majnun) and the addressee of her poem, who is presumably her husband, to the female (Layli).

29. The notion that "real" love, whether erotic or spiritual, transcends particular religious denominations is a convention of Persian poetry.

30. Silver is a common epithet for skin in Persian poetry, but here it perhaps refers to white hairs in Mastureh's husband's beard.

31. As in Mastureh Kurdi's poem "We've gone, we left behind us . . ." (p. 101), mystical love is seen as something that transcends orthodoxy (the mosque) and blasphemy (the wine shop and the—Hindu or Buddhist; in Persian pre-modern texts the two are often conflated—temple). In Persian poetry religious/mystical ecstasy is quite often compared to drunken dancing, with the implication that "normal" categories of good and bad behavior, the secular and the religious, the orthodox and the blasphemous, have been superseded.

32. Dogs are considered to be unclean in Islam, and to pollute whoever comes into contact with them. The convention behind the poem is that a lover haunts his or her beloved's alleyway like a stray dog, and one meaning can be that the poem's speaker is implicitly comparing herself to the despised dog. By contrast, the beloved is compared to the sun. The poem also has an implied spiritual dimension: the sun is like God, who shines on all alike, whether noble or

despised (as you—the beloved—should shine on me, no matter how contemptible you find me).

FROM THE 1800s TO THE PRESENT

1. For further commentary on Tahereh, see the Introduction, pp. xli–xliii.

2. This poem has been attributed to other poets as well as Tahereh, although the consensus is that it is probably Tahereh's. The fact that the last lines include the poet's name is not decisive, as this could have been added later by a copyist.

3. The poem is addressed to the Bab, Tahereh's spiritual leader, although in terms of the traditional rhetoric of Persian mystical poetry, much of it could also be read as being addressed to God; the ambiguity is deliberate. The poem's tropes and metaphors—wine, drunkenness, the replacement of the speaker's self by the object of passion, being burned by love, being drowned in a sea of gnosis, the equivalence of various religious traditions, the dust of the beloved's street being like the Moslem ka'bah for the speaker, and so on—are all stock features of Persian mystical poetry, though Tahereh's passionate deployment of them reads as a rhetorical tour de force.

4. In Islamic lore, Christ's breath could revive the dead; here a kiss, rather than simply breath, is implied.

5. The ka'bah is the black stone in Mecca at the center of Islam. As in many Persian poems concerned with love, erotic or spiritual, the equivalence of different religious traditions is implied.

6. A Christian version of the beloved as the qebleh (see note 27 on p. 249, for "Flute-like, while you're away . . . ," p. 100).

7. Mahsati (p. 7) was the most famous woman poet from before the nineteenth century, and Shahdokht is claiming that she is the "Mahsati"—the outstanding woman poet—of her time.

8. The poem celebrates the poet's wedding night. The comparison of a beautiful body to flowers of various kinds was a customary trope in Persian poetry from its earliest beginnings. Tulips are a conventional metaphor for blood and the phrase "My lap was filled with tulips" (line 5) almost certainly indicates bleeding consequent to her hymen being broken, as this evidence of the loss of virginity was traditionally considered to be an important aspect of the wedding night.

9. This poem has also been attributed to other poets, including Tahereh (p. 109). A number of pre-modern women poets boast of their beauty in extravagant terms. This pride in one's beauty seems to be a female equivalent of the way pre-modern male poets often boasted about their unrivalled poetic prowess.

10. Both the Bible (Exodus 4:6) and the Qor'an (27:12) mention the miracle of God ordering Moses to withdraw his hand from his cloak, which appears to be preternaturally white when he does so.

11. This world and the world after death.

12. The images in the poem (Majnun, the nightingale, the moth, the wine, the pourer and the glass) are associated with worldly, physical love, but the poem's subject is almost certainly mystical love.

13. Jamshid and Kay Kavus are legendary pre-Islamic kings, and wine in poetry is often associated with the pre-Islamic era.

14. The most beautiful rubies were said to be from mines in Badakhshan, in northeastern Afghanistan.

15. That is, "You've confused the ideal and the actual—fantasy and reality."

16. This poem was written during the turmoil of the Constitutional Revolution (1905–11), in response to a patriotic poem by the poet Eshqi (1893–24).

17. Heaping earth on the head is a metaphor for mourning (since this was done literally by mourners in the past).

18. In this line and subsequently, "you" refers to Iran.

19. Cyrus is the pre-Islamic king Cyrus the Great (c.600–530 BCE), who founded the Achaemenid empire; Feraydun and Kay Qobad are legendary pre-Islamic kings who appear in Ferdowsi's Persian epic the *Shahnameh* (completed in 1010 CE).

20. Anushirvan (501–79 CE) was a Sasanian king, famous for his justice.

21. Nader (1688–1747) was one of the most powerful rulers in Iran's history; he spent virtually his whole adult life engaged in warfare, which is why Jannat mentions his "saber."

22. Though the poem is a response to a particular event in the First World War, Nimtaj brings in other more general themes that were widely discussed at the time. These include an implicit anti-monarchism (in the figure of Kaveh), a reproach by women to Iranian men for being unable to defend their country, and contempt for those

men who say that women should remain veiled and absent from public affairs.

23. The story of Kaveh appears in Ferdowsi's *Shahnameh*. He is a blacksmith who leads a successful rebellion against the demonic, foreign (Arab) king Zahhak. Because of his status as a plebeian outsider to the royal court, populist political movements in Iran have frequently taken him as a prototypical proletarian rebel.

24. The decisive battle in 636 CE, in which the Arab Moslem forces defeated the army of the last pre-Islamic dynasty, the Sasanians. This event is regarded ambiguously in Persian literature, as it was the battle that destroyed the pre-Islamic Iranian empire, but it was also the means by which Islam came to the country. Nimtaj is emphasizing the positive aspect of the battle, the fact that the Moslems triumphed.

25. Andalusia, Spain; the province was Moslem from 711 CE, when it was conquered by an Arab army, until 1492, when it finally fell to the Christian monarchs Ferdinand and Isabella. It was thus Moslem for considerably longer than it has since been Christian.

26. "They" in the previous line and "you" here refer to men.

27. Orumiyeh (two lines above) and Salmas are both towns in Azerbaijan, in northwest Iran, that were briefly overrun and sacked as a result of a Kurdish attack backed by Ottoman forces, during the First World War.

28. For further commentary on Alam Taj, see the Introduction, pp. xlvi–xlix.

29. The word Alam Taj uses for "chamber" means literally a bridal chamber, so that the line can also be read as meaning "Would that they'd perish in their bridal

chamber," that is, that death would be preferable to marriage.

30. For the first few lines this looks as though it will be a typical "praise poem" about the poet's husband, but it soon becomes apparent that far from praising her husband the poem is a satirical attack on him.

31. The major epic of Persian literature, completed in 1010 CE, much of which celebrates Iranian warrior-heroes and their military victories.

32. Nader Shah, a warlord who seized the Iranian throne in 1736, and overran Delhi, which his army sacked in 1739. See note 21 on p. 253.

33. Rostam, the chief hero of the stories of the legendary section of the *Shahnameh*.

34. Alexander the Great (see next note). Dara, the name in Ferdowsi's *Shahnameh* of the king known in the West as Darius III.

35. In Islamic lore, Alexander is regarded as a kind of proto-Sufi, whose journeys were undertaken in search of wisdom as much as for the sake of conquest. It's an exaggeration, though, to imply, as Alam Taj does here, that he is seen as a prophet.

36. Sa'd ibn Abi Waqqas was the Arab commander at the Battle of Qadesiyeh (636 CE), which marked the end of the Sasanian empire.

37. The capital of the Sasanian empire, situated on the Tigris, close to modern-day Baghdad. The "Persian general" who led the Iranian forces at Qadesiyeh was Rostam-e Farrokhzad (not to be confused with the legendary Rostam). In his *Shahnameh* Ferdowsi presents him as someone who knows that the forces against him are

invincible but who chooses to fight on nevertheless. It's not clear what the "general's fatal flaw" in the next line refers to; perhaps simply his pessimism as to the battle's outcome.

38. The Islamic period in Iran began with an Arab defeat of the country's last pre-Islamic dynasty, and Iranian culture has always had an ambivalent attitude toward Arabs and their civilization; intensely patriotic Iranians sometimes think of Arabs as Iran's natural enemies. Throughout the nineteenth century, England and Russia contended with one another for control of Iran, and both countries have been cordially loathed by many Iranians ever since this time. The Ottomans were the chief enemy of the Iranian Safavid dynasty (1501–1736), and an uneasy enmity between the two states lingered for long after this period (as in the Kurdish–Ottoman incursion into Iranian Azerbaijan mentioned in the poem by Nimtaj Salmasi on p. 128).

39. The name of Alam Taj's parents' family cook.

40. The *Maqamat* is a medieval collection of Arabic stories and the *Maqulat* a commentary by Ibn Rushd (Averroes, 1126–98) on Aristotle's *Metaphysics*. Both were used as Arabic teaching texts.

41. This Aristotelian distinction is elaborated in Ibn Rushd's *Maqulat* (see previous note).

42. In common with some other women poets (e.g., Parvin Etesami, p. 143), Alam Taj wrote a number of poems to household objects (as well as this poem to her samovar, she addressed poems to her sewing machine, her comb, her mirror, and her curling iron). It's difficult to read these poems without being aware of the profound loneliness, both literal and spiritual, that seems to lie behind them.

43. Both "ancient den" and "wretched hovel" (five lines below) refer to the world.

44. Dust was traditionally poured or smeared on the head during ritual mourning, and "dust upon the head" became a phrase meaning a state of extreme grief. "Dust upon your head" is a fairly common curse in Persian.

45. For further commentary on the life and work of Parvin Etesami, see the Introduction, pp. xlvi, xlviii–l.

46. This poem is said to refer to Parvin's brief marriage, which ended after ten weeks when she returned to her father's house. She is reported never to have mentioned the marriage again, except perhaps obliquely in this short poem.

47. Didactic dialogue poems involving non-human characters like these (usually animals or birds, but sometimes aspects of nature or inanimate objects) were a specialty of Parvin Etesami. Verse dialogues of this kind are a conventional Persian form, one that was augmented in Etesami's case by her familiarity with the verse fables of Jean de La Fontaine (1621–95). A Western reader will probably assume that the poem is primarily about race relations, and it may well be, but it comes out of a tradition of Persian poems that assert a shared human identity that transcends sectarian religious (rather than perceived racial or ethnic) differences.

48. This poem is often attributed to Parvin Etesami, though it's not certain that it is hers. Armenians are of course Christians.

49. Parvin Etesami is emphatic in her obvious anger at the traditionally inferior status of women in Iranian society. The reforms of Reza Shah (r. 1925–41) that began to redress women's grievances occurred during her lifetime,

and the poem welcomes these reforms. In common with a number of other female poets of the late nineteenth century and early twentieth century who were concerned with women's social status, Etesami emphasizes the importance both of women's education and of women acting in ways that would ensure their opinions would be taken seriously. She can be particularly condemnatory of women whose behavior reinforces cultural stereotypes about women being empty-headed scatter-brains; this accounts for the way that, as the poem continues, she seems to backtrack a little from the implication in the first stanza that women's inferior status was entirely due to society's patriarchal structure.

50. Brushwood is gathered as fuel for a fire.

51. A reference to spinning, which was seen as the archetypal "task" for a woman, particularly one who was poor.

52. The expression "to drink blood" means "to suffer."

53. The Persian New Year falls at the spring equinox (March 20 or 21), and it is usual at this time to buy and wear new clothes.

54. A "black crow" was a traditional metaphor in pre-modern Persian poetry for disaster or evil. Here its primary meaning is death.

55. Houris are the beautiful angels who welcome the faithful into the Islamic paradise; Ahriman is the Zoroastrian principle of evil. Persian poetry commonly mixes references to different religions in one image (here the image refers to the sun emerging from the darkness of the night).

56. The metaphor is a Sufi commonplace, though here it is given a secular meaning. Like many other women

of her time, Etesami saw access to knowledge and the acquisition of an education as the prerequisites of women's emancipation.

57. For further commentary on Zhaleh Esfahani and her fellow poets, see the Introduction, pp. lv–lvi.

58. A free-verse version of the fable-dialogue genre frequently used by Parvin Etesami, as in her poem "White and Black" (p. 144).

59. The title of this poem in Persian means "ingratitude" colloquially, though etymologically it derives from a word meaning "blasphemy" and both meanings are implied in the poem, perhaps the etymological meaning more than the colloquial one.

60. The mountain chain to the north of Tehran.

61. The river that runs through Esfahan, the poet's birthplace.

62. An alternative version of "Zayandeh Rud," the name of the river that runs through Esfahan.

63. The Iran–Iraq war of 1980–88. Estimates of total casualties vary from one million to twice that number.

64. A reference to the time of the Pahlavi monarchy, which could be notoriously arbitrary in its appropriation of others' property (hence "plunder"); the "sly nightwatchman" is Mohammad Reza Shah (r. 1941–79), exiled by the Islamic Revolution in 1979.

65. For further commentary on Simin Behbahani, and her friendship with fellow poets Lobat Vala (p. 174) and Forugh Farrokhzad (p. 179), see pp. li–lvi.

66. Traditionally in Persian poetry, tearing one's clothes and biting the back of one's hand are gestures that indicate extreme emotion (which can be either positive or negative).

67. "The book" is Rumi's (1207–73) major work, the *Masnavi-ye Ma'navi*.

68. As she grew older, Simin Behbahani became progressively blind, and these images refer primarily to her gradual loss of sight, but they can also be taken as referring obliquely to the problems of the social/political situation she faced.

69. The whole poem is about the Iran–Iraq war of 1980–88 and its aftermath.

70. For further commentary on Lobat Vala and her friendship with Simin Behbahani and Forugh Farrokhzad, see the Introduction, pp. li–lii, liv–lv, lvi.

71. The poem was written in Paris, as is indicated in the books by Lobat Vala in which it has appeared; just as it has for many American and British visitors, Paris has tended to suggest the glamor of romance and (perhaps illicit) love affairs for Iranians too.

72. The Simorgh is a mythical bird that appears in medieval Persian poetry. In Farid ud-Din Attar's *The Conference of the Birds* (twelfth century) it represents God, which is probably its primary meaning here. The "Friend" is another way, common in medieval and later poetry, of referring to God.

73. For further commentary on Forugh Farrokhzad and her friendship with Simin Behbahani (p. 164) and Lobat Vala (p. 174), see the Introduction, pp. lii–liv.

74. The title poem of her first book. The poem came out of the self-questioning that preceded her leaving her husband and the breakup of her marriage.

75. Part of the force of the poem is that in pre-modern Persian poetry one kind of ring (an earring) was indeed the mark of slavery.

76. For further commentary on Tahereh Saffarzadeh, see the Introduction, pp. lviii–lix.

77. This poem is dated two months after the return of Ayatollah Khomeini to Iran in February of 1979, which marked the beginning of the Islamic Revolution. At this time the walls of the main cities, especially Tehran, where Tahereh Saffarzadeh was living, were covered in political slogans and graffiti.

78. The "family" refers to the Ghaznavid dynasty, who began as slaves and rose to rule an empire, centered on the city of Ghazni in eastern Afghanistan, which conquered much of Iran and northern India in the first years of the eleventh century.

79. Balkh is in northwest Afghanistan, Nayshapur and Bayhaq (now called Sabzevar) are in northeastern Iran, and Bokhara is in modern-day Uzbekistan.

80. A large oasis south of the Aral Sea. The English form of the name used to be Chorasmia (Shelley referred to "the lone Chorasmian shore" in his poem *Alastor*, l. 272).

81. Khwarazmi (ninth century) and Biruni (tenth–eleventh centuries) were both polymaths and scholars.

82. Among the most important Persian-language poets of the tenth and eleventh centuries.

83. Prominent members of the Ghaznavid court; Bayhaqi is best known for his *History*, which is one of the major works of early Persian prose.

84. The story of Hasanak, a vizier of the Ghaznavids in the eleventh century, who was accused of treason by a rival (Maymandi) and executed, is told in Bayhaqi's *History* (see previous note); in Persian culture, the incident has become emblematic of intrigue, betrayal, and the ingratitude of

princes. The poem traces the dynasty's slave-to-emperor narrative, and its paradoxical mixture of greatness, sophistication, brutality, and betrayal.

85. A pre-Islamic hero whose tale is told in the major Persian tenth-century epic the *Shahnameh*; he is emblematic of the betrayed stoic young hero who is innocent of the accusations made against him, one of which eventually brings about his death.

86. Mariam is Mary, the mother of Jesus; "gnostic" can imply both that she is in touch with the divine, but also that she is aware of her son's future fate.

87. The biblical Rachel, the wife of Jacob (in the Qor'an, Yaqub); the "fourteen years" is the time in which she waited for news of her son Joseph, who had been sold into slavery by his brothers. Persian poetry often refers to Yaqub's sorrow during this period; a reference to his wife's sorrow, as here, is much more rare.

88. The woman known in the Bible as Potiphar's wife. Her illicit love for Joseph is a major theme in Persian poetry, often given a mystical interpretation.

89. In Islamic belief, Hagar is the second wife of Abraham and the mother of Esmail (Ishmael); at the prompting of Sarah, Abraham's first wife, she and her son are abandoned by him in a stony waterless desert.

90. Among the earliest Iranian poets (both tenth century); Rabe'eh is the first poet represented in this book.

91. Nakisa was a celebrated female harpist and composer at the court of the pre-Islamic king Khosrow II (d. 628 CE).

92. Khosrow Parviz is another name for Khosrow II (see previous note).

93. A male musician at the court of Khosrow II; he and Nakisa collaborated as joint supervisors of the court's music.

94. Ferdowsi (940–*c*.1020), Iran's most important epic poet, author of the *Shahnameh*. The "noble epic meter" refers to the meter of the *Shahnameh*, which became standard for epic verse after Ferdowsi's use of it.

95. Avicenna, or Ibn Sina (980–1037), philosopher, astronomer, and physician.

96. Atossa (550 BCE–475 BCE) was a daughter of the Achaemenid king Cyrus the Great and the wife of the first King Darius (r. 522 BCE–486 BCE); for much of her life she was the power behind the Achaemenid throne.

97. Jamshid is a mythical king whose story is told near the opening of the *Shahnameh*; his "arrogance" refers to the fact that he thought himself equal to God, and lost his throne as a consequence.

98. Hafez (*c*.1315–*c*.1390) was the major lyric poet of Iran.

99. Bayhaqi (995–1077) was one of the most important of Iran's early historians. (See note 83 on p. 261.) The *Masnavi* is the major long mystical poem of Mowlavi/Rumi (1207–73), sometimes referred to as "the Qor'an in Persian."

100. Shams was the wandering dervish who is said to have been decisive in Mowlavi's commitment to Sufism.

101. In both Moslem and Christian tradition this refers to a group of young men who in order to escape religious persecution hid in a cave where they slept for 300 years before waking and emerging from their hiding place.

102. Farhad is a figure in the romance "Khosrow and Shirin," by the poet Nezami (1141–1209). A mason in love with Shirin, the wife of King Khosrow, he wounds himself

with his own tools when he hears the false news that she has died, and commits suicide. (See note 19 on p. 248.)

103. A traditional symbol of blood in Persian poetry.

104. The cities of Nayshapur and Balkh and the provinces of Khorasan and Khwarazm were among the first places to be annihilated during Genghis Khan's invasion of Iran, which began in 1219.

105. This is the third of three poems dealing with war. Kobane is a mainly Kurdish town in the north of Syria that was besieged by ISIS forces in 2014. The capture of the town and its surrounding villages caused the flight of an estimated 400,000 refugees.

106. The words "celebrity" and "selfie" (stanza 2), "placards" (stanza 3), and "feminists" (stanza 4) are in English in the original poem.

107. The Iranian poet Hafez (*c.*1315–*c.*1390) and the American poet T. S. Eliot (1888–1965).

108. Gregor Samsa, the protagonist of Franz Kafka's *Metamorphosis* (1915).

109. The anti-war novel published by Kurt Vonnegut in 1969.

110. A reference to *The 120 Days of Sodom*, the novel written by the Marquis de Sade in 1785.

111. Tribute: literally *"zakat,"* alms—a religious tax on wealth.

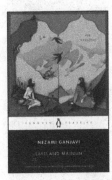

LAYLI AND MAJNUN

Nezami Ganjavi

Translated with an Introduction and Notes by Dick Davis

The iconic love story of the Middle East, by a Persian poet who has been compared to Shakespeare for his subtlety, inventiveness, and dramatic force, *Layli and Majnun* tells of star-crossed lovers whose union is tragically thwarted by their families and whose passion continues to ripple out across the centuries.

SHAHNAMEH

Abolqasem Ferdowsi

Translated by Dick Davis
Foreword by Azar Nafisi

This prodigious narrative tells the story of pre-Islamic Iran, beginning in the mythic time of creation and continuing forward to the Arab invasion in the seventh century. One of the greatest translators of Persian poetry, Dick Davis presents Ferdowsi's masterpiece in an elegant combination of prose and verse.

ROSTAM

Abolqasem Ferdowsi

Translated with an Introduction by Dick Davis

No understanding of world mythology is complete without Rostam, Iran's most celebrated mythological hero. This titan of magnificent strength bestrode Persia for five hundred years and owed allegiance only to his nation's greater good. Anyone interested in folklore, world literature, or Iranian culture will find *Rostam* both a rousing and an illuminating read.

 PENGUIN CLASSICS

Ready to find your next great classic? Visit prh.com/penguinclassics

FACES OF LOVE

Hafez, Jahan Khatun, Obayd-e Zakani

Translated by Dick Davis

Together, Hafez, a giant of world literature; Jahan Khatun, an eloquent princess; and Obayd-e Zakani, a dissolute satirist, represent one of the most remarkable literary flowerings of any era. Acclaimed translator Dick Davis breathes new life into the timeless works of these three masters of fourteenth-century Persian literature.

VIS AND RAMIN

Fakhraddin Gorgani

Translated with an Introduction by Dick Davis

Against a background of court intrigue and conflict, Vis finds herself escorted to her future husband, King Mobad, by his brother, Ramin, who falls in love with her and jeopardizes their fates. Considered the first Persian romance and the inspiration for *Tristan and Isolde*, this masterpiece is a timeless story of forbidden and dangerous love.

THE CONFERENCE OF THE BIRDS

Farid Attar

Translated by Afkham Darbandi and Dick Davis
Introduction by Dick Davis

Composed in the twelfth century, Farid Attar's great mystical poem describes the pilgrimage of the world's birds in search of their ideal king, the Simorgh bird. The most significant of all works of Persian literature, this masterly translation preserves the poem's rhymed couplet form and nuances of language.

PENGUIN CLASSICS